Hollywood is a strange country where appearance is reality that feeds the dreams and fantasies of the gay soul like no other city. This memoir reveals the comic rise and operatic fall of West Hollywood author Larry Townsend, the "Liege Lord of Leather," whose *Leatherman's Handbook* was a founding text for gay men worldwide in the 20th century. What Townsend wrote in 1972 describing his own iconic *Handbook* applies to *Drummer* editor Fritscher's 2021 handbook about Townsend: "…a definitive exploration of the gay S&M leather scene…written by a qualified writer who has observed it all from the inside." If you are an old hand at leather, or new to the kink scene, this candid memoir offers a fascinating, witty, and authentic true story of leather lives lived the way we were, and were forced to be, from the 1950s to 2021.

Review Comments

Who better than longtime leather author Jack Fritscher of *Drummer* fame to write a fast, fun, and fact-based account of early LA leather life as lived by the great Larry Townsend in this frank and charming memoir that raises questions such as "Where was the world's first leather bar?" As a leather publisher, I think fans of Townsend will enjoy this well-told movie-like Hollywood backstory of how and why Larry wrote *The Leatherman's Handbook* that "helped create the very leather culture he reported on."
—**Dave Rhodes, publisher,** *The Leather Journal*

The Leatherman's Handbook remains a legacy guide for young S&M leatherfolk wanting to learn the way we were. Larry Townsend, who fought to protect the rights of authors and artists, was one of the most ethical and honest people I have had the pleasure of knowing. This is the Hollywood story of how he lived and how he died on Sunset Plaza Drive, five minutes from Sunset Boulevard.
—**Durk Dehner, co-founder, Tom of Finland Foundation**

Jack Fritscher lights up our Leatherworld skies in this West Hollywood memoir of his boisterous friend and collaborator, the

Grand Leather Master Larry Townsend who came out in the world's first leather bar, and taught generations of leatherfolk how we might live. The fast-turning pages reveal the rise and fall of Townsend's roller-coaster life. Fritscher, who invited Townsend to write for *Drummer*, is the perfect eyewitness in this authentic story of pioneer leather lives.

—**Peter Fiske, author,** *My Leather Life: Early Years*

In this lively memoir of writer, photographer, and pleasure activist, Larry Townsend, Jack Fritscher elevates this biography of his longtime friend by blending memories, anecdotes, and Townsend's work at *Drummer* for an expansive view of the man, his times, his frustrations, and his impact on his community. Fritscher celebrates this key figure in the leather/kink world not by putting him on a pedestal, but by capturing him in all his full unvarnished glory, and in doing so makes a significant contribution to an often-overlooked chapter of LGBTQ history.

—**Owen Keehnen, author,** *Leatherman: The Legend of Chuck Renslow*

Larry Townsend's was the kind of brilliant life often canceled by puritans who devalue people who contribute to the sexual pleasures some of us dare to explore. I am thrilled that Larry's friend and fellow giant, Jack Fritscher—editor of *Drummer* magazine, author of twenty books, and muse to Robert Mapplethorpe—has written this awesome pop-culture memoir to remind leatherfolk of Townsend's importance to our history, and how much we owe to him for today's freedoms. Fritscher's writing is passionate, dazzling, and downright fun to read. What a life! What a book!

—**Thor Stockman, producer,** *S/M at the Movies: The Good, The Bad, and the Ridiculous,* **New York**

Larry Townsend's *The Leatherman's Handbook*, a unique amalgam of research, erotica and advice, was something of a founding text for the gay SM and Leather subculture of the late 20th century. Jack Fritscher's memoir of Townsend, and his pioneering social circle, is a wide-ranging, anecdotal insider's look at the West Coast Gay Lib and Leather scenes from the 1970s to 2008. Larry Townsend—author, researcher, advice columnist, and political

activist—has been something of an unknown quantity in LGBT writing to date. Not any more! Jack Fritscher knew the old Master for many years. He has served him well!
—**Ian Young, author,** *The Male Homosexual in Literature* **and** *Encounters with Authors: Essays on Scott Symons, Robin Hardy, and Norman Elder*

I really do love this book. Only the legendary Jack Fritscher could have written this engrossing, richly detailed remembrance of the equally legendary Larry Townsend. Who else could seat us at a restaurant table in West Hollywood to eavesdrop on bickering leather pioneers gesturing with steak knives? Jack's affection for Larry is palpable on every page, even when he recounts having to upbraid him over a misbegotten lawsuit. Much of the memoir centers on Townsend's fraught on-off relationship with *Drummer* magazine; its scheming publisher John Embry; and its LA editor, Larry's fickle "Leather Wife," Jeanne Barney. What emerges is an intimate, engaging, briskly paced, behind-the-scenes portrait of one towering figure, a master of literary leatherotica and nonfiction, told by another towering figure in homomasculine literature and culture. This memoir will cement both Townsend's and Fritscher's position forever in the upper echelon of the pantheon of homomasculine leather cultural icons.
—**Hank Trout, senior editor,** *A&U: Art & Understanding* **("America's AIDS Magazine"), and editor,** *Drummer* **(1980)**

Over the past fifty years, Larry Townsend's writings about sex and BDSM have touched generations of kinky people, even those who today may not know his name. To them his friend Jack Fritscher offers the inside story of the legendary influencer's rise and fall. Through a mix of archival documents and photos, Fritscher puts us next to Townsend as he, his friends, and his rivals move through and, in many cases, establish the worlds of gay publishing, politics, and leathersex. Fritscher's lively, propulsive text reveals the private man struggling behind his public persona, even as he fights for the rights of other independent authors. In our culture that tries to separate the struggle for human rights from the sex lives of the people demanding those rights, Townsend's uncompromising advocacy and unsanitized writing remind us of what we are fighting for, and Fritscher's act of friendship returns him to us.

 —**Nayland Blake, artist, educator, curator,** *Tag: Proposals on Queer Play and the Way Forward*, **The Institute of Contemporary Art, Philadelphia**

Jack Fritscher does it. Again. In this fascinating new memoir, he does for his iconic friend Larry Townsend what he did in his best-selling memoir of that other sexual outlaw, his lover Robert Mapplethorpe. This fast-moving and entertaining West Hollywood story dishes up to the reader a vivid portrait of the larger-than-life Leather Guru Townsend by recounting their forty years of friendship against all odds. An acute observer of human nature and gay pop culture, Fritscher seems the perfect insider to intrduce readers of a new generation to the complex and politically-incorrect influencer whose important and seminal *Leatherman's Handbook* taught the 20th-century gay world about leather and kink culture while he fought for the rights not only of the leather/BDSM community, but of writers, artists, and the LGBTQ community in general. I enjoyed this wonderful book immensely. A very welcome addition to the literature of LGBTQ leather history and of LGBTQ history in Los Angeles.

 —**Lester Strong, special projects editor,** *A&U: Art & Understanding* ("America's AIDS Magazine"), **and writer, "blu sunne" blog at blusunne.com and aumag.org**

In 2008, shortly before leather icon Larry Townsend died, Jack Fritscher wrote to him about a new-guard magazine "that leaves old fucks like you and me (nothing personal but we are both so last midcentury) out of the new DNA of the changing leather LGBT picture." Fritscher's memoir offers old and young leatherbears alike an insightful and lavishly illustrated retrospective about the man who helped define queer leather life for as long as this old fuck can remember. Most importantly, we are given the chance to witness Larry's life firsthand as experienced by one of the great masculinst authors of our time.

 —**Ron Suresha, author,** *Bears on Bears: Interviews & Discussions* **and** *Fur: The Love of Hair*

Only the bravest embark on authoring a history of a publicly misunderstood and overlooked community. In *The Life and Times of Larry Townsend*, Jack Fritscher, again, establishes himself as a cultural scholar who can impact an entire movement by not only writing about the present but also by writing about the past. Townsend's *The Leatherman's Handbook* created an undeniable impact, and Fritscher preserves it by narrating the cultural context and shift that surrounded it. This memoir is more than a tale of two friends bound in leather. It's a road map documenting an entire movement and takes readers into a loop of a time gone by. I learned so much.
 —**August Bernadicou, historian, The LGBTQ History Project, lgbtqhp.org**

Comments Previous Work

"*Drummer* editor Jack Fritscher and his books are unabashed and uninhibited tour guides."
 —**Chuck Renslow, Founder, Leather Archives & Museum, and International Mr. Leather (IML)**

"Jack Fritscher writes wonderful books...careful writing...a world of insight."
 —**Geoff Mains, author,** *Urban Aboriginals*, **in** *The Advocate*

"Veteran author Jack Fritscher is an anarchist of gay sexual prose, the man who invented the South of Market prose style (as well as its magazines...). Fritscher writes with sweat and wit."
 —*The Bay Area Reporter*, **San Francisco**

"Jack Fritscher is a prolific writer who since the late Sixties has helped document the gay world and the changes it has undergone."
 —**Willie Walker, founding member, GLBT Historical Society, San Francisco**

"Jack Fritscher reads gloriously."
 —**San Francisco Chronicle**

Larry Townsend, age 20, self-portrait, 1950, shot shortly before he volunteered for the U.S. Air Force and served as Staff Sergeant in charge of NCOIC Operations of Air Intelligence Squadrons with the U.S. Air Force in Germany (1950-1954).

The Life and Times
of the Legendary

Larry Townsend

Author, *The Leatherman's Handbook*
27 October 1930 – 29 July 2008

A Memoir

On the 90th Anniversary of His Birth
and the 50th Anniversary
of *The Leatherman's Handbook*

Jack Fritscher, Ph.D.

Archival Edition
Jack Fritscher-Mark Hemry Archives

Palm Drive Publishing™

Copyright ©2021 Jack Fritscher
All rights are reserved by the author. Except for brief passages quoted in newspaper, magazine, radio, television, internet review, or other electronic media, or academic paper, no part of this book may be reproduced or transmitted in any form or by any means, electronic or mechanical, including photocopy, recording, web posting, or any information storage-and-retrieval system now known or to be invented, without permission in writing from the publisher.

For author history and for historical research www.JackFritscher.com

Cover and book design by Mark Hemry
Front cover photograph by Larry Townsend
Back cover photograph by Mark Hemry

Published by Palm Drive Publishing, Sebastopol CA
www.PalmDrivePublishing.com
Email: publisher@PalmDrivePublishing.com

This memoir is a product of the author's recollections and is thus rendered as a subjective accounting of events that occurred in his life. This is a memoir book of humor, comedy, and satire meant to refract the author's eyewitness experience of what might otherwise be objective history.

Library of Congress Control Number: 2021939197
Fritscher, Jack 1939-
The Life and Times of the Legendary Larry Townsend / Jack Fritscher
p.cm
ISBN 978-1-890834-99-9 Print
ISBN 978-1-890834-53-1 eBook

1. Biography/Autobiography. 2. Personal Memoir. 3. Homosexuality. 4. Masculinity. 5. Gay and Lesbian Studies. 6. Gay Studies (Gay Men). 7. Popular Culture. 8. Editors, Journalists, Publishers. 9. Sadomasochism. 10. American Literature—20th Century. 11. Feminism. 12. Homomasculinity.

First Printing 2021
10 9 8 7 6 5 4 3 2
PalmDrivePublishing

Dedication

To the memory of Larry Townsend
with gratitude to Jeanne Barney
for her eyewitness testimony
and to my husband and editor Mark Hemry
without whose remarkable diligence
over forty-two years this historic material
would have been impossible
to collect, analyze, and present

The Sexual Revolution
of the Titanic 1970s

Epigraph

They were careless people, Tom and Daisy
—they smashed up things and creatures and
then retreated back into their money or
their vast carelessness or whatever it was
that kept them together, and
let other people clean up the mess they had made.
—F. Scott Fitzgerald, *The Great Gatsby*

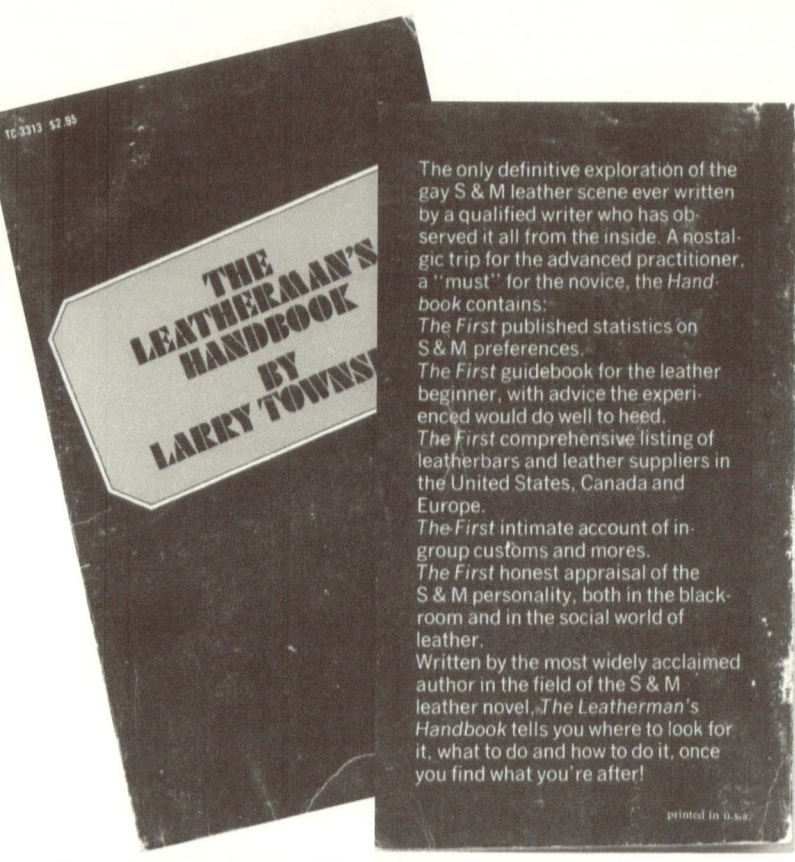

First edition. Back cover. The author described his book as: The only definitive exploration of the gay S&M leather scene ever written by a qualified writer who has observed it all from the inside. A nostalgic trip for the advanced practitioner, a "must" for the novice, the *Handbook* contains:

- *The First* published statistics on S&M preferences.
- *The First* guidebook for the leather beginner, with advice the experienced would do well to heed.
- *The First* comprehensive listing of leather bars and leather suppliers in the United States, Canada, and Europe.
- *The First* intimate account of ingroup customs and mores.
- *The First* honest appraisal of the S&M personality, both in the black-room and in the social world of leather.

Written by the most widely acclaimed author in the field of S&M leather novel, *The Leatherman's Handbook* tells you where to look for it, what to do and how to do it, once you find what you're after!

Contents

1	Thirteen Years after Larry	1
2	An Origin Story	4
3	Preppie, Sergeant, Sex Tourist, Leatherman	7
4	First Gay Writers Summit, San Francisco 1970	11
5	The Name Game	15
6	Coming Out Twice	18
7	Larry's Golden Age: Stonewall to AIDS	23
8	Loud Gay Silence	29
9	One-Handed Reading: Erotica or Porn?	34
10	A 10-Inch Pound of Flesh	40
11	Blacklists and Grudge Matches to the Death	44
12	The Conservative Dilemma	47
13	Hanged, Drawn, and (French) Quartered	59
14	Jeanne Barney	68
15	Larry's "Leather Wife"	77
16	Litigious Larry: Is a Lawsuit Harassment?	82
17	Coming Out in 1950s Los Angeles	85
18	Townsend and Embry Rivalry	91
19	Sex Perversion, Fellatio, and Entrapment	95
20	Lifelong Community Volunteer	99
21	He Who Dies with the Most Column Inches Wins!	102
22	The King Lear of Leather	105
23	Author Declares War on Bookstores	112
24	Suddenly That Summer: June and July 2008	119
25	Last Brunch at Casa Del Mar	125
26	The Email Letter: Drop That Lawsuit!	130
27	The Passion and Death of Larry Townsend	134
28	From The *Drummer* Salon to *Honcho*	145
29	A Montage Recap	146
30	The Townsend-Yerkes House	149
31	Illustrations	151

Los Angeles Times, April 14, 1955
UCLA Student Gets Medal for Rhine Heroism

Irvin T. Bernhard, 24, UCLA sophomore [name later changed to "Michael Lawrence 'Larry' Townsend," July 19, 1972], was presented with a medal and scroll yesterday by Dr. Richard Hertz, German Consul General in Los Angeles, for saving a 9-year-old German boy from drowning in the Rhine River at Bonn last August.

Gov. Karl Arnold of the German state of Nordrhein-Westfalen sent the scroll and medal to Dr. Hertz for presentation to Bernhard, who was a member of the U.S. Air Force when he performed the heroic feat.

The youngster had been riding along a Rhine River road on his scooter when he had an accident and fell into the deep river. As a swift current spun the boy around in the water, Bernhard, who was eating at a nearby sidewalk café, got up, raced to the river, and dived in fully dressed.

"I swallowed an awful lot of the Rhine, but the two of us made it back to shore all right," Bernhard, who lives at 624 Veteran Avenue, West Los Angeles, recounted yesterday in the German Consulate at 3450 Wilshire Blvd. Accompanying the young man to the Consulate was his sister, Mrs. Ralph J. Tingle of 621 S. Barrington Avenue, who proudly looked on as Dr. Hertz gave the awards.

Los Angeles Times, April 14, 1955. "UCLA Student Gets Medal for Rhine Heroism" In Germany in 1954, Staff Sergeant Larry Townsend of the U.S. Air Force, age 24, jumped fully clothed into the Rhine River to save a boy from drowning. It was the kind of pro-active heroism that typified his character, his writing, and his life.

1

THIRTEEN YEARS AFTER LARRY
HIS 90th BIRTHDAY
THE 50th ANNIVERSARY OF
THE LEATHERMAN'S HANDBOOK

Thirteen years after Larry Townsend's death, I am writing this valedictory memoir about my friend on his ninetieth birthday and the fiftieth anniversary of his *Leatherman's Handbook* which was the first analysis of leatherfolk in the twentieth century. For all the praise around his legend, no one has yet bothered to study his life, his writing, or his historical context. No one has mounted exhibits of the photos he shot, or of the hundreds of erotic drawings and photographs he commissioned as a gay arts patron to illustrate his publications. At age 82, I am writing about this writer, this activist, this man in full, warts and all, from my personal experience of him and of his big booming voice which I am quoting from his own vintage words folded inside yellowing periodicals, nostalgic letters, fading faxes, and recorded phone conversations.

 I'm not exposing anything secret here about him or his inner circle of *Drummer* editor Jeanne Barney, *Drummer* publisher John Embry, film director Roger Earl, and film producer Terry Legrand, because in life, and in business on page and screen, these exhibitionists, always acting out, lived large in plain sight, and doubled-dared anyone to make a crack. While I'm diving deep in this memoir, in this dissonant Hollywood musical-comedy, I could, in fact, dive deeper into my memory and archives, but these people who were my friends are too recently deceased to go there in this "quantum writing" that folds time elliptically while repeating a few stories to stir in spiraling new facts and feelings each time with more *Rashomon* information. This apologia for them contains an apology to them. Because I am a fallible human writing about other fallible humans, I wish my commemoration to give the benefit of the doubt to all the living and dead. So what I opine in this memoir I write allegedly. Didn't Chaucer, grown old, ask forgiveness for any slights in his *Canterbury Tales*? I'm just a documentarian letting the found footage play, like Magnus Bishop, the pop-culture professor, who is the narrator of my novel *Some Dance to Remember*.

After the Stonewall Riot changed gay character in 1969, its aggressive violent energy, affecting Larry, swept virulent through gay culture igniting the divisive gay civil war that began at the Stonewall Inn and continues to this day in politically-correct cancel culture over who and what is authentic, proper, and kosher enough to represent gay folk. For instance, gay literary criticism is often twisted by all kinds of purity tests around politics, sex, race, and gender. For all its vaunted equality and diversity, it is often applied exclusively, arbitrarily, and without nuance. Can politically-correct thinking cancel critical thinking?

Larry Townsend as avatar and victim is a case in point of "who gets to march in the Pride Parade." The gay literary establishment that recruits diversity had no place at the table for gay folk-author Townsend, and little understanding of his hearty gay pop-culture literature that spoke authentically to the psyche at the heart of male homo*sex*uality. To his credit as a psychologist and healing mentor, he dared champion consensual sadomasochism as an empowering analgesic ritual for men trying to cope counterphobically with PTSD caused by exposure to lifelong homophobia.

San Francisco novelist Frank Norris wrote: "A literature that cannot be vulgarized is not literature at all." *Vulgar* means *popular* in the same good way the Vulgate Bible stories were written as accessible pulp-fiction for ordinary people. In literary reckonings, Larry tried to shrug off the insult that his best-selling pop-art vulgate novels were squeezed out of the gay canon, but a draft up your kilt is always cold.

Canons are a construct of social engineering. Canons rarely open. Canons stay stodgy because of competitive passions over incoming reputations and politics, as well as over ages-old bourgeois fears that formerly illegal adult subject matter and vocabulary, no matter how brilliant or essential, will somehow taint the polite literary canon, lose arts funding, threaten classrooms of innocent students, and ruin the reputations of publishers, bookstores, and journals that acknowledge it. You know. *Ulysses. Lady Chatterley's Lover. Howl.*

The canon of American pop music rejected rap before accepting a vulgate art form that is as essential to Black culture as literary erotica is to gay culture. S&M literary erotica is to mainstream gay literature what tough-and-sexy film noir is to mainstream Hollywood studio family fare. Like the named genres of "Gay Mysteries" and "Gay Sci-Fi," this genre, often historicized as "Gay Pulp Fiction," might be more distinctly dubbed "Gay Literotica" or "Gay Leatherotica."

Thanks to scholars of progress and balance, there is a post-Stonewall reclamation effort around "lost" LGBT Literotica. One champion of this genre of gay American literature is Harvard professor Michael Bronski who thanked Larry Townsend for his help in gathering research material for Bronski's nonfiction book, *Pulp Friction: Uncovering the Golden Age of Gay Male Pulps.* In his "Introduction," Bronski wrote that while reclaiming

> this literature can only have positive effects on how we view the queer past, there is also a danger that these books could become part of what is referred to as the gay canon. This would be a terrible, and I think, unhealthy fate.... the idea of a "gay canon" is not only unnecessary but unhelpful. In his essay, "The Personal Is the Political," Edmund White notes, "I myself am in favor of desacralizing literature, of dismantling the idea of a few essential books, of retiring the whole concept of a canon."

Larry on the West Coast would have said to these East Coast gatekeepers. "Yeah. Yeah. Yeah. Nice theory." But in practice, he wanted in the door.

This is a memoir, and only that, of a man who helped create the gay culture that drove him mad.

2

AN ORIGIN STORY
LIFE AS A MOVIE
THE ASTROLOGER'S WARNING

Larry Townsend, the charismatic author of the classic 1972 *Leatherman's Handbook*, died at 2:40 Tuesday afternoon, July 29, 2008, at Cedars-Sinai Hospital in Los Angeles. Born Scorpio with Aries rising on October 27, 1930, in Jackson Heights, Long Island, he was 77 and HIV-negative when he was overcome by complications from pneumonia. Defining an era and a literary genre, he was one of the gay pioneers who changed the post-Stonewall fin de siècle of the twentieth-century. He was an urgent author in whose work fans saw the evolution of themselves in a performative S&M lifestyle. For over forty years, after meeting on February 13, 1963, he lived with his lover-partner, Fred Yerkes (August 27, 1935 – July 7, 2006), in the Hollywood Hills above the Sunset Strip and below the iconic white Hollywood Sign, the symbol of Los Angeles ambition, sex, politics, backstabbing, and dreams.

Two months after his birth, his mother in their five-room home on the top floor of 35-63 80th Street, Apt. 6A, Jackson Heights, New York, where he was conceived, paid for an astrology-like "Old Gold Broadcast Character Reading" that was answered with a three-hundred-word profile predicting her newborn son's destiny.

> December 18, 1930...After studying your name... you're a lucky boy! Men in your group frequently become financial and scientific leaders. I do hope you won't neglect your splendid abilities. You have good judgement, a fine mind, wisdom beyond your years, tolerance toward the

views of others...but I urge you not to get in the habit of tyrannizing over your friends....You like to see people and money working for you....Your name and destiny combination...should not be changed....Petty trifles annoy you...Your type...often marry after 25....Do not change your name. Sincerely, Lorna Fantin

But change his name he did. And his destiny. He was a person of his own creation. He was a force of nature and of will. Introducing his identity and image to readers during the dawning of the Age of Aquarius, he wrote in 1970 that he was a very sexual "Scorpio with Aries ascendant." At that time in gay popular culture, the number one pick-up line in a bar was "What's your sign?" Writing for forty years under his primary pseudonym "Larry Townsend," Irvin Townsend "Bud" Bernhard, Junior, authored dozens of novels including *Run, Little Leather Boy* (1968), *The Faustus Contract* (1969), *The Fairy King* (1970), *Beware the God Who Smiles* (1971), and the gay heritage guide *The Leatherman's Handbook* at such erotic presses as Greenleaf Classics and the Other Traveller imprint of criminal literary thief Maurice Girodias's Olympia Press.

Larry dedicated his *Handbook* to, among others, Canadian writer Ian Young who had started his own gay publishing company in 1970 and authored *The Male Homosexual in Literature*. Young made a pop-culture point when he wrote that these early publishers were churning out sexually explicit pulp fiction in cheap paperbacks with deliciously lurid titles and succulent covers that in lieu of reviews in a then non-existent gay press sold the books—and have since become collectible gay pop art.

Larry's *Run, Little Leather Boy* with scenes in castle dungeons in Southern Germany was a famous bestseller—and a private catch phrase. When the thin-skinned Larry would get royally pissed off over some person, some issue, or some slight, and would sometimes threaten thunderbolts, we'd sometimes dare tease him back to good humor—and to get him to tone it down—by stage-whispering at him, "Run! Little Leather Boy! Run!" which, of course, made him so mad he couldn't help but laugh at how (during his whole life) he let his emotions in his private life be buoyed up or stressed by public responses to his politics, his writing, and his prized reputation as a dashing author in our gay Vanity Fair.

The Advocate, a tad wary of the sex in *Run*, reported on June 23, 1971:

> Despite its very clear exposition and vivid descriptive passages, the sensitive undertones of this story reflect Mr. Townsend's background as a graduate psychologist and student of human behavior. It also suggests an intimate knowledge of a subject [S&M] in which he is already an acknowledged authority.

3

PREPPIE, SERGEANT, SEX TOURIST, LEATHERMAN

As Larry's family moved from New York to Boston to Los Angeles, he grew up as a big-boned blond boy of Swiss-German heritage a few houses from Noel Coward and Greer Garson. He ate cookies with his neighbor Laura Hope Crews who played "Aunt Pittypat" in *Gone with the Wind*. At age fourteen in 1944, during World War II, he entered the elite Peddie School in Hightstown, New Jersey, a non-denominational college-preparatory boarding school near Princeton where, before girls were admitted, he wrote for the school paper, swam in the pool known as "the bathtub," and was nursed in the school infirmary by the long-serving and coincidentally named matron Miss Eva Townsend.

During World War II, the Peddie School was mobilized as an airplane spotting post with students like Larry acting—so like a Townsend sex story—as air-raid wardens keeping 24-hour watch against Nazi invasion. As wartime students came and went with military service during his four years there, his schoolmates in grades nine through twelve plus post-grad, included liberal Democrat Dick Swig who became the owner of the Fairmont Hotel in San Francisco, and the conservative Republican author Richard Hornberger who later, after serving as a surgeon in the Korean war, took the pen name Richard Hooker and wrote the 1968 novel, movie, and television series, *MASH*, just as Larry was writing *The Scorpius Equation*. It was that kind of school, and he graduated in 1948 marked with the education he received.

In 1950 at age twenty, he photographed himself—a portrait of the artist as a young man—in a brooding black-and-white head-shot. He staged it framing himself against a writer's filing cabinet topped with a bondage padlock. He intended it as his passport photo into the literary world of authors. He was a freshman at the University of California Los Angeles, and was about to join the Air Force. He was impeccably groomed, poised, and beautiful the way the young are beautiful.

From 1950 to 1954, he was stationed as Staff Sergeant in charge of NCOIC Operations of Air Intelligence Squadrons with the U.S. Air Force in Germany. In the election for president in November 1952, he voted Republican for Dwight D. Eisenhower and Richard M. Nixon. In August 1954, he saved that German boy (who would now be seventy-five) from drowning in the Rhine River, finished his military service, and returned to the University of California Los Angeles (UCLA) as a sophomore on the G.I. Bill.

Having cruised in the closet of his car since his teen years, he came out to his own formal satisfaction in 1955 at the primeval LA bar, Cinema, on Melrose Avenue which was likely the world's first leather bar, predating the Argos leather bar founded in Amsterdam in 1957, Chuck Renslow's Gold Coast leather bar in Chicago in 1958, and the Why Not and Tool Box leather bars in San Francisco in 1962. The dive was perfect for him and the new gay motorcycle clubs, like the Satyrs founded in 1954, hosting mixers for sadists and masochists who were also military veterans. In his "Introduction" to his *Handbook*, he describes the Cinema interior and action in detail, saying it was "what a leather bar should be."

During his European service, he, whose father was a spy during World War II, worked with spies and spying. He told me he was lucky that, while he was stationed at Essen, a civilian bisexual who graduated Cambridge and was a Fulbright scholar, figuring Larry was gay, tutored him in discretion, and introduced him to reading such as Gore Vidal's 1948 novel *The City and the Pillar*.

Traveling on his own more often in mufti than uniform, Larry, who based so many of his novels on historical people and epochs, day-tripped wandering through Europe on his motor scooter soaking up culture, food, and drink while reading around in sadomasochistic literature in quiet cafés and *bierstubes*. His knapsack on his back was a traveling library of books like Sacher-Masoch's *Venus in Furs* which he praised with passing mention of Gilles Deleuze in his *Handbook*, Jean Genet's *Our Lady of the Flowers*, and Pauline Réage's just-published *Story of O*. If he could spy for the Air Force for underground Nazis, he could spy for himself. So he set out gathering useful "leather intelligence" about sex dynamics in gay boltholes like public toilets—all later reported in *The Leatherman's Handbook*.

Gathering intelligence ran in his family. He showed me his 1950s government "Personnel Security Questionnaire" in which he explained he had not been a child-spy for the Wehrmacht:

> While on duty with USAF Intelligence Service (7050th AISW, Rhein Main ABF), my secret clearance was revoked for a period of approximately two weeks, due to the fact that my father (Irvin T. Bernhard, Sr.) had been active in collecting information for the FBI on German Bundest activities in New England during 1940. His name had been recorded on some subversive list at that time. A letter from J. Edgar Hoover, instructing him as to field offices and indicating that his help was appreciated is on file with security office, SDC. Also, refer to Mr. J. Frank Mothershead, 5241 42nd Street NW, Washington. D.C. This gentleman is former head of Patent Law Division, Dept. of Justice, and is aware of details to greater extent than I, since I was only ten years of age at the time.

Mustering out after his closeted tour of duty, he came out into a world of available men at UCLA before coming out into the 1950s underground of the LA gay scene where he and Hollywood star Montgomery Clift, who sported a wicked leather jacket in *A Place in the Sun*, shared a lover. That romantic triad ended when Clift, fresh off shooting *Suddenly Last Summer*, spirited the ham in their sandwich away to Cuba for the wild New Year's Eve before Fidel Castro marched his revolution into Havana on January 8, 1959.

In the mid-1960s, Larry began photographing some of his leather partners for a scrapbook he continued most of his life, and for illustrations in the many magazine-size S&M short-story booklets he published in addition to his pocket-novel books. Always prepared, he kept rolls of film and a loaded camera on a tripod in his dungeon. His accounting parallels the *Stud Files* that erotic novelist Samuel Steward began keeping on his rough-trade tricks at the suggestion of Dr. Kinsey in the 1950s.

With his degree in industrial psychology from UCLA (1957), he began several years' work in the private sector as a probation officer at a juvenile camp managing teenage delinquents shaped by 1950s rebel teen movies and rock-n-roll. As a counselor he had undergone the therapy required to advise others, but, he told me, he could find no guilt in himself about his own proclivities. During his forty-four-year home-relationship with his partner Fred Yerkes, a wisp of a lovely man who died two years before him in 2006, the S&M master was a committed animal lover favoring Doberman Pinscher dogs whom he called his "Doberpersons," and Abyssinian cats who were the only creatures ever really able to top him.

4

FIRST GAY WRITERS SUMMIT, SAN FRANCISCO 1970
SONG OF THE LOON AND GAY LUNATICS
GAY MAIL-ORDER WEBS GAYS TOGETHER

Famous in the Swinging 1960s, years before the Stonewall rebellion in 1969, the political, prolific, and best-selling Larry was so respected by his peer-group authors that Richard Amory, who conceived the meeting, invited him to join the first gay-pulp-fiction writers summit in San Francisco on June 15, 1970. This authors' self-defense meeting was called at the same moment that the gay albino founder of Guild Press, the dysfunctional Lynn Womack, went to jail for printing photos of underage models after ten years of publishing dozens of gay 1960s novels for his Black Knight Classics line distributed by his Guild Book Service mail-order. This was at the expense of authors he held hostage like Sam Steward whose 1965 novel *$tud* Womack scandalously withheld from publication out of meanness while he hid out in a hospital to dodge his exploited authors. In gay history, this was ten years before the seven Violet Quill writers in Manhattan separated their literary selves from the pop genre of "gay pornography" and met for the first time to power up their own East Coast writers literary co-op in New York.

   Larry drove from Los Angeles to meet the current San Francisco local authors for a panel discussion at the SIR Center, hosted by the Society for Individual Rights. This was the first time he met his host Amory who cloned his *Song of the Loon* trilogy out of Rousseau's mythic homomasculinity of the Noble Savage in James Fenimore Cooper's *Leatherstocking Tales* in which frontiersman Nattie Bumppo—clad in leathers and traveling with his Mohican brother/lover, garbed like half the Village People—scouted new American frontiers just as these writers were doing.

Amory introduced Larry to his fellow pre-Stonewall authors such as Sam Steward whom I had just met in 1969, Richard Fullmer, Peter Tuesday Hughes, and Douglas Dean who all admired his aggressive entrepreneurship, his sturdy marketing, and his best-sellers in a growing market where a total short stack of some thirty gay pulp paperbacks published in 1965 tripled to a hundred in 1966 and exploded to more than five hundred before Stonewall in the transformative year 1969 when gay director John Schlesinger's movie of the 1965 gay novel by James Leo Herlihy, *Midnight Cowboy*, despite its homophobic X-Rating, won the Academy Award for Best Picture. Larry listed Herlihy and John Rechy as required reading in *The Leatherman's Handbook*.

Fullmer told Drewey Wayne Gunn at *Lambda Literary* on August 10, 2011, that he considered 1960s underground gay "dirty books" to be the "fertilizer" that nurtured the mainstream gay literature that followed. (Insert your own joke here.) In truth, these were men on the verge of a hybrid gay literature that was often both prurient and literary in their books that were illegal. These authors, all constantly threatened with arrest for writing their outlawed novels, looked to political activist Larry for ideas to resist arrest by police, exploitation by publishers, and persecution by puritans.

Dissatisfied with publishers' corporate greed around royalties and copyrights, the writers convened to discuss founding a gay publishing collective to be named the Renaissance Group. God knows, it was needed. As a young author in 1969, I sent my first S&M novel, with its first line a literary homage to the first line in *Studs Lonigan*, to Greenleaf publishing, but refused its offer of $300 for the manuscript and all rights everywhere forever. When Frances Green, the editor of the Other Traveller gay series for Olympia Press, read of Larry's San Francisco meeting, she invited the attending writers to send their manuscripts to her. Between 1970 and 1972, she and a second woman, Ginger Sisson, published many book titles with Greenleaf Classics in San Diego, including thirteen by Larry who was paid a flat thousand dollars per title, with no royalties, before Olympia went out of business letting his *Handbook* go out of print.

In the Townsend storyline, Larry lived as he died, stating his truth. Twenty-eight years after he began fighting for justice like a superhero around his literary rights in 1970, he died mad as hell in a raging firestorm of his own making in his lawsuit against gay bookstores and a publisher that tarnished his legacy in 2008.

Because in 1970 there was no gay publishing entity worth suing, and no court gay-friendly enough to hear such a case anyway, he channeled his frustration into action by starting his own boutique mail-order publishing house, LT Publications, in 1972, the same year the straight world was shocked open by the erotic art of *Last Tango in Paris*, and John Waters—whose first short film was 1964's *Hag in a Black Leather Jacket*—broke free of Hollywood studios and released his independent film *Pink Flamingos*. Larry wrote more with purpose than passion. His writing was his activism. In October 1971, he explained in *Vector*, the monthly magazine of the Society for Individual Rights (SIR) in San Francisco:

> Literary contracts in the porno market are virtually meaningless. There's no way to force payment, because attorney costs and court fees will exceed anything you could hope to recover....I have found it necessary to make one cardinal rule: *Don't give anything away* [his italics]. Like any professional, the writer's most (only) valuable asset is his time. Except for the writing I do for H.E.L.P. [Homophile Effort for Legal Protection], which happens to be a cause [bailing out gay men entrapped by the police] in which I strongly believe, I do not write anything unless I get paid for it. I have a couple of pen names I use for straight, nonfiction articles and stories. I have several *noms de plume*...[Always marketing his small business like self-publisher Walt Whitman, he, like Walt, wrote many of his own reviews. Calling himself "Peter Lovejoy," he reviewed his own *Sexual Adventures of Sherlock Holmes* "as a spoof, a burlesque," in proto-*Drummer* 1, issue 2, December 1971.] I keep a constant flow of

short pieces going out all the time. This supplements the income and also allows me a break from the novels, which are my principal love. If I didn't do this, there would be periods of starvation between those of affluence.

Defying the astrologer's 1930 warning about those many 1960s pen names, he also changed his birth name from "Irvin Townsend Bernhard, Junior" to "Michael Lawrence Townsend," reprinted his *Handbook*, and took control of his art and business life. With that name-change decree issued by his attorney Vance Gary Prutsman on July 19, 1972, when Irvin—who as a teen called himself "Bud"—became Larry, he established his identity and brand, and broke free from corporate book publishers.

As an independent writer-photographer working from home, he created his LT Publications, and earned his worldwide reputation as a reliably consistent publisher of Leatherotica literature that made bookstore cash registers ring. He trusted in the sexual infinity of leather to give him both content and readers. He disrupted the vertical monopoly of incestuous corporate publishers crushing down from the top decreeing to subordinate imprints what authors may be published as was allegedly acted out later in corporate synergy when the media group, Liberation Publications, which owned *The Advocate*, bought Alyson Press whose books *The Advocate* reviewed. Even the benevolent Lambda Rising Bookstore in D.C. ran both the *Lambda Literary Review* and the *Annual Lambda Literary Awards*.

Journalist Liz Highleyman wrote in her syndicated "Past Out" column in the *Seattle Gay News* that "critics [were] warning about an impending LGBT media monopoly." Against such vertical corporate synergy, Larry offered instead a rebellious and practical alternative showing how the horizontal power of independent publishing liberates and levels the playing field where the free originality and full diversity of all voices can be published.

5

THE NAME GAME
HOLLYWOOD BABYLON

The post-Stonewall cultural revolution, a mix of Marx and Mao, found queer sport in hunting out "alias" identities because plainclothes detectives and gays who were police informants used fake names which, because of deception, was not cool, especially in gay bars where nicknames, like drag names, were often needed as a common self-defense for privacy. Larry, the former military spy, was attacked for his "double identity" by gay political opponents as if his pen name becoming his legal name somehow invalidated his integrity in liberation politics as president of H.E.L.P. As the astrologer predicted, his challengers did not like him tyrannizing over them, nor did they appreciate his Thor-like thunder of Germanic anger over trifles. (His Swiss half, he said, was neutral.) Perhaps his critics did not yet know that midcentury gay men Thomas Lanier Williams became Tennessee Williams and Truman Streckfus Persons became Truman Capote and Touko Valio Laaksonen became Tom of Finland.

His friend "J. R."—most likely John Rowberry who succeeded me as the third editor of *Drummer*—wrote in the hybrid *H.E.L.P.Drummer* in May 1973:

> Larry has been attacked for not using his "real" name..."Michael Lawrence Townsend" has been his legal name since he became involved in the Movement. I know, because I went through all the soul-searching with him...I suggested that he go through a legal change of name, since he never liked his first name, anyway, and "Townsend" was his middle name....I think this was the most liberating thing he could do. It marked a complete

cut with the closety past and left him free to do or say whatever he wanted without involving his family....

Because Larry Townsend, a master of dominance and submission, noted that mainstream gay history characteristically separates and suppresses alternative leather history, especially the erotic, to keep it invisible and unexplored by means of its withering vanilla gaze, it is worth citing that he ran his West Coast book publishing house for five years before novelist Felice Picano pioneering in Manhattan founded his indie SeaHorse Press in 1977, and then in 1980 became a founding member of the Violet Quill along with Andrew Holleran—the pen name of Eric Garber—and with Edmund White who said on the *Lambda Literary* site in 2013 that Holleran's *Dance from the Dance* (1978) was a brand new portrayal showing "gay men living among gay men," which was, more accurately, the exact kind of male-bonding portrayal Larry had been dramatizing in his novels since 1969 and *Drummer* had been publishing since 1975.

While these mostly New Yorkers may have suggested they were founders of modern gay writing, there already existed, besides the agitated agitator Larry Kramer, a litany of a hundred midcentury LGBT novelists, nearly all using pen names. Mary Renault, Patricia Highsmith, Ann Bannon, Rita Mae Brown, and Patricia Nell Warren were already frontrunners alongside Sam Steward, James Barr, James Baldwin, James Purdy, James Leo Herlihy, John Coriolan, John Rechy, Gore Vidal, Carl Corley, and Larry Townsend.

As a writer and photographer, Larry was an essential eyewitness of the drama performed around *Drummer* in which his novels were sometimes excerpted next to the educational advice and self-help columns he contributed starting in 1980.

Contrary to myth, Larry Townsend was not a founder of *Drummer*. However, along with Robert Mapplethorpe, and Robert Opel who streaked the 1974 Academy Awards, Larry Townsend was a charter member of the sex, art, and salon around *Drummer* which helped invent the very leather culture it reported on. "I'm not a *Drummer* writer," he wrote of himself:

I'm a novelist whose books were often excerpted in *Drummer*. In 1978, Jack Fritscher, the new editor of *Drummer*, took me to supper [in San Francisco] and began to convince me over pasta [at the Haystack restaurant, 3881 24th Street] that the San Francisco *Drummer* of the late 1970s was a different *Drummer* than Los Angeles *Drummer*. [As founding San Francisco editor-in-chief, I strengthened, virilized, and darkened *Drummer* which had been born blond in LA.] After many more months of Jack's friendly persuasion, I came on board because so many of the fans of my books were also *Drummer* subscribers.

6

COMING OUT TWICE
THE NEW JOURNALISM
FACT AND FICTION IN
THE LEATHERMAN'S HANDBOOK

Larry not only covered gay issues, he focused attention upon them. In *The Advocate*, March 26, 1975, three months before the first issue of *Drummer*, Larry was the first person to explain to the world of mainstream vanilla sex that leatherfolk must come out twice: once to sex, once to fetish.

> I have heard all of these liberationists speak about their concern for the young person who emerges as a gay human being within an outwardly hostile world. They are concerned for his (or her) ability to survive without the support of other...groups or persons who share this sexual orientation. They should be doubly concerned with the dilemma of a person who must first go through the trauma of accepting himself as a homosexual, and then cope with his S&M proclivities. For him (or her)... the coming out process is two-fold and fraught with twice the number of pitfalls.
>
> Practiced intelligently and with a degree of moderation, S&M can provide a tremendous catharsis. It can allow the participants to discharge an enormous amount of pent-up emotional tension. By the same logic that we justify a gay relationship on the basis of its being healthier to do it than to abstain and suffer the emotional consequences of deprivation, so I believe it is better for the sadomasochistically oriented person to act out these

impulses with a willing partner than to stifle the whole in a quagmire of guilt.

I have been asked to speak on this subject at several universities and other academic gatherings, but [to this date, 1975] I have consistently declined after doing it twice and experiencing the difficulties involved. Explaining any emotional condition to a group of people who do not share these emotions is the proverbial situation of describing color to a blind man.

Books are clones of the author. Larry did not need to make door-to-door house calls at universities. His *Handbook* was such a years-long bestseller that he literally educated American and international gay popular culture about the nature of leather people, principles, and practice. In Europe in 1977, *Der Spiegel* reported that in the world scene of leathermen, "*The Leatherman's Handbook* by a certain Larry Townsend is considered their Bible." He was an entertaining teacher who was not didactic, prescriptive, or old guard.

He stated directly in his *Handbook* that he was writing no more than his opinion based on his experiences:

> Your desires may exceed or fall far short of the action I describe. This is exactly how it should be. No one—not Larry Townsend or anyone else—can even begin to set the standards for your sexual needs and/or behavior.

As a psychologist who wrote novels as a business, he fluffed up the abstract ideas in his *Handbook* with seductive episodes of erotic fiction because sex sells. He took a cue from Helen Gurley Brown's best-selling self-help handbook, *Sex and the Single Girl* (1962). He studied San Francisco leatherman William Carney's *The Real Thing*—an epistolary novel of leather mores and manners published in 1968 in which a seasoned leather master, inspired by Pierre Choderlos de Laclos' sado-maso *Les Liaisons Dangereuses*, writes instructive and seductive letters of advice to a young leather supplicant. Larry frothed up the facts and fictions from his own experience and from guys who shared with him the facts and fantasies of midcentury leather life as it was lived as the 1960s became the 1970s.

He used a pyramid scheme to create his *Handbook*. His collection of leathermen's oral histories was a gay-history first. In 1969, he composed a "Leather Fact Sheet" questionnaire that he as social scientist, psychologist, and marketing guru developed and mailed out like a chain letter to a hundred men across the nation. Each guy was asked to make five copies and mail them along to five friends. I remember my longtime intimate, the Catholic leather priest Jim Kane, gave me a copy in 1969 which I retyped onto a mimeograph stencil and mailed to my friends with Larry's return address at the top. The questions themselves were so provocative that the joke was we all jerked off at the questions while writing our real and fantasy answers.

The mail began pouring in addressed, as was one, to "Master of Masters, Larry, Sir." For many in that new Stonewall era, the Q&A was their first act of gay liberation. This was the exact time the homomasculine cowboys in *Brokeback Mountain* were struggling to come out in Annie Proulx's short story about masculine-identified men. Larry was delighted at the detailed answers enhanced with the extravagant personal experiences and fantasies that men added. The Q&A format worked so well in 1969-1971 that in 1981-1982, he sent our 6,000 questionnaires for *The Leatherman's Handbook II*.

Absorbing all these men's voices into a narrative, Larry, half reporter and half novelist, joined the trending wave of New Journalists like Truman Capote in *In Cold Blood* (1966) and Hunter Thompson in *Hells Angels* (1967). Writing as a very unique participant insider, he mixed fact and fantasy, and activated gay publishing with erotic interactivity. What other gay book has so changed behavior, given permission for a lifestyle, and made grown men sit up and beg for more? In his leather reading list in the *Handbook*, Chapter 15, "Literature," he recommended the work of Truman Capote. So is his *Handbook* in which he admitted "fictionalizing" perhaps a bit of a nonfiction novel?

Larry was a skilled ventriloquist who openly admitted he made nearly all of his *Handbook* up. He meant he processed all the incoming information through his own mind's eye. He explained the sources of his diverse fictive voices in chapters 2, 11, and 15, revealing that he most often wrote from the masochist's point of view because readers identified with it more than with the sadist's. He disclosed how he transposed gay men's voices into his own omniscient narrative voice. They gave him and his *Handbook* text—echoing them—the visceral authenticity that causes readers to suspend disbelief while taking the text as gospel truth guiding their own potential lives that they must uncloset to become their own identities layered in homosexuality, leather, and sadomasochism. He disclosed:

> If you recognize my "style" [his quotes] in the narrative [letter(s) he is printing], it happened because the gentleman writing the letter was a better S than he was a writer. My editing became a little heavy-handed.... In my own case, for instance, a large part of my leather writing has been in the first person, told through the eyes of an M. For this reason, I have had many top men approach me, assuming this is my scene. It really isn't...in *fictionalizing* [Italics added] these stories, it is simply much easier to describe a wide range of experiences....[Identifying with the Marquis de Sade, he observed the fantasy distance between an author's imagination and his actual experience.] As the poor bastard [de Sade] spent most of his life in prison [like leathermen locked in the mid-twentieth-century closet], he had much more time to dream and write than he had to act out his fantasies.

In terms of the 1970s zeitgeist, at the same time Larry's readers were discovering *The Leatherman's Handbook*, they were also reading San Francisco author Robert Pirsig's 1974 advice-novel *Zen and the Art of Motorcycle Maintenance* which, like Larry's *Handbook* was a fictionalized true story more about instilling values than about either Zen or motorcycles.

Townsend was the first mentor to many kinky men and women, and the third-person Oracle in many leather couples' relationships. His healthy counsel in his gay men's adventure stories activated thousands of men who wrote to him thanking him for helping them to understand S&M psychology, and to come out into their natural-born temperaments. The way he jumped into the Rhine River to save the drowning German boy, he saved many a gay man from drowning in tears.

7

LARRY'S GOLDEN AGE: STONEWALL TO AIDS POLITICS AND PLAGUE THWART STUDIES OF THE LIEGE LORD OF LEATHER
GAY LITERARY HISTORY CANNOT LOOK AWAY

When the Psychedelic 1960s exploded in a glitter bomb at the 1969 Stonewall riot, gay character changed. Larry seized the 1970s before AIDS changed us again in 1981. His articles of revolution and novels of revelation became textbooks for students learning leather culture. During the ten glorious years of sexual freedom after the publication of *The Leatherman's Handbook* in 1972, Larry became the liege lord of leather. He changed gay sexuality by offering S&M as a rite of male passage in a politically-correct decade dismantling the role of paternal parenting. He paved the leather runway for *Drummer* magazine, Robert Mapplethorpe, and gay S&M films while creating audiences for them all by schooling the taste, and affirming the fancies, of millions of leatherfolk.

When the 1970s rolled over to the 1980s, credentialed critics began publishing articles about the Townsend effect on gay culture, but AIDS all too quickly sucker-punched the positive scholarship gaining momentum around his provocative work. Some vanilla gatekeepers desperately seeking a scapegoat to sacrifice or a witch to burn screamed that S&M sex caused the plague. In 1985, *Drummer* issue 87 quoted one critic, John Lauritsen, a member of the Gay Liberation Front since 1969, who preached that poppers, stereotyped by many as an essential S&M drug, caused AIDS. *Drummer* 99 rebutted him by quoting Dr. Bruce Voeller, the man who coined the phrase "Acquired Immune Deficiency Syndrome" and who wrote that anti-popper crusaders were often too politically motivated to discuss the issue.

Suddenly, Typhoid Larry and Sam Steward, and all us leath-erotica authors had our thousands of published pages virtually burned by fundamentalist queer reactionaries who otherwise before HIV had marched against censorship and discrimination. Frankly, I didn't go out looking for the Gay Liberation Front as an antagonist in this memoir, but everywhere I turned in Larry's archive, there it was in clipping after clipping. Even so, there is joy to be found in many other early critiques. In the *Philadelphia Gay News*, 13, April 16-29, 1982, poet Ian Young, author Sam Steward, and college lecturer Brandon Judell wrote about Larry, leather culture, and the psychology of S&M.

Ian Young in his essay, "S&M: The Initials Also Stand for Sex Magic," assayed the rise of cancel culture while explaining S&M relationships and the magical thinking that sustains gay sex. He made a point about S&M serving the gay psyche: "Gay relationships, simply because there are no social models, can create themselves out of their own needs." As an eyewitness, he peeled back the intramural gay civil war waged against "politically incorrect" S&M identities and desires and literature by judgmental mainstream vanilla gays and Marxist leather gays whose power trip is blacklisting, censoring, and shaming writers like Larry. Young, even though he wrote that "Larry's scene and approach are different from mine," made his point specific:

> John Rechy is in town, to debate about S&M....He's against it. Like most opponents of S&M, Rechy links it with Hitlerism. Does he believe it? The S&Mers I know are for the most part as politically conventional as everyone else....It used to be alleged that all homos are Commies. The Communists described homosexuality as "the fascist perversion." But "fascist" now means anyone of whose politics or activities the speaker strongly disapproves. Virtually all attacks on S&M are repeats of non-gays' attacks on gays. The same illogic, the same emotional hyperbole, the same earnest repetition of untruths....
>
> S&M is primarily erotic theater. Its aim is pleasure-giving and therapeutic: It offers assimilation of

experiences that in "reality" might be very unpleasant but which have attractive erotic elements. S&M extracts the erotic elements and acts them out in a reasonably safe context.....The elements of drama, play, and magic are essential to S&M. They are essential to us as human beings, and in a world which allows fewer and fewer outlets for these aspects of creativity, S&M is becoming more popular—like horror movies, mountain climbing, "Dungeons and Dragons." But S&M also involves a coming to awareness of different levels of the self, a revelation, and a sharing. I mentioned the idea of magic. For me, that's the third meaning of the letters S&M: sadist/masochist; slave/master; sex/magic.... I write from time to time on S&M, and, I hope, help people untangle their own thoughts about it. But I don't want to be put in a position of "defending" S&M, anymore than I want to "defend" being gay.

My friend Sam Steward (1909-1993) liked to pay to kneel to straight sailors, cops, and Hells Angels he took to the backroom of his tattoo parlor. He scorned what he lamented was gay leathermen's cheap imitation of real-world domination and submission. At his cottage in Berkeley where he loved playing the role of Grand Old Man, he'd ask me, "What are they up to on Folsom Street?" I'd tell him. He'd say, "That's the end of everything." While he liked Larry and wished his own alter-ego Phil Andros had written a bestseller like *The Leatherman's Handbook*, Sam insisted on debunking the 1970s leather scene as less authentic than his own underground S&M sex scenes that began as the Roaring 1920s crashed into the Depression that made hordes of hungry blue-collar trade available for hire. "Buddy, can you spare a dime?" Sam paid for sex. Larry paid for models.

In 1964, four years before he heard of Larry, Sam had published his essay, "The Leather Fraternity: Boys Looking for 'Real' Men," which *Philadelphia Gay News* reprinted in 1982. As the author of the 1953 novel, *The Motorcyclist*, Sam cracked wise about the evolution of leather culture from the war-torn 1940s to the hippie 1960s which were the life and times when Larry had come out. Sam showed how necessary it was for some sage like Larry to come along and make safe the ways of bike boys on the prowl:

> In the early fumbling days of the [leather] "movement" that was not a movement then, when there were still a few real men around, the S&M game was dangerous and exciting. If you then found a guy, back in the late 1940s, who wore a leather jacket and boots and had sideburns and looked at you with narrowed eyes, you knew he was the real McCoy—probably a jackroller with a real motorcycle, a heterosexual, who might tie you up and beat the hell out of you, rob you—even kill you. If you met the guy in the 1950s, dressed the same way, you might find that he was a homosexual, perhaps sadistically oriented, and that by now he had lost his motorcycle, and had only the costume. You were still taking chances; if you handed him a whip, he might seriously injure you, or burn you, or leave you tied up too long until gangrene set in. But if you meet the same guy in the leather bars in the 1960s, there's no way of knowing what he is, or who does what to whom, unless it's pre-arranged...[which was the main reason why the leather action in the 1970s switched in self-defense to the safe spaces of baths like the Barracks and Slot and clubs like the Mineshaft where cruising crowds of witnesses could monitor the wild free-for-all scenes].

Brandon Judell in that issue offered a humorous genuflection to Larry in "Why S&M Is Just a Pain in the Ass to Me."

> I cannot recall having conscious S&M fantasies until a Philadelphia expatriate presented me with Larry Townsend's *The Leatherman's Handbook*.... Unto this very day I envisage being a beautiful cop getting plowed by a bunch of gay bruisers (see Townsend's chapter on gang bangs). Townsend's other tales, supposedly true, were enjoyable but not my cup of Celestial Seasonings.... At that point, with my thumbed *Handbook* deteriorating

along with my morals, the owner of a national chain of greeting card stores introduced me to *Drummer* magazine [while I happened to be editor]. Without any warning, I was masturbating more often than Ronald Reagan naps. I was "Prison Punk." [A story by Frank O'Rourke] I exercised in the "S&M Gym." [A serialized novel by G. B. Misa] My supple flesh was being shaved and...

Karla Jay, the first woman president of the Gay Liberation Front, and Allen Young revealed in their 1979 book of interviews, *Lavender Culture*, how specific the midcentury war against male S&M culture could be among early members of the GLF in New York whose separatist attempt at gender recalibration was the reason Larry openly condemned the GLF in *H.E.L.P.Drummer*, March 1973. They quoted radical feminist John Stoltenberg, husband of the dour anti-porn militant Andrea Dworkin, saying:

> Anti-sexist genetic males might also find useful *Double F: A Magazine of Effeminism*, issue 2, 1973, in which Steven Dansky, John Knoebel, and Kenneth Pitchford repudiate "sado-masculinity" [Larry's specialty] and "masoch-eonism" [male transvestism] with reference to the sexism of the gay liberation movement.

Forty years after that, I met Effeminist founder Steven Dansky when he interviewed me for his video series *Outspoken: Oral History from LGBTQ Pioneers*. Dansky was an early roots member of the Gay Liberation Front. As we became friends, we compared notes on our misspent youths. He told me about his time in the Left as documented in Linda Hirshman's book *Victory: The Triumphant Gay Revolution*:

> While working at a left-wing bookstore in the late Sixties, later GLF stalwart Steven Dansky remembers being given instruction in how to cross his legs and hold his cigarette so as not to appear effeminate and lose his chance at going to Cuba to meet his revolutionary brothers.

Dansky never expected these electric issues of gender to follow him into early gay liberation, as it was known at the time, but there was enormous tension in GLF between the femmes and butches that to some extent, he said, accounted for the demise of the organization.

Talk about the power of the underground press. The authoritative voice in Dansky's magazine, made credible, like Larry's, by the very act of indie publication, seemed to represent a popular movement with a substantial readership supporting the agenda when, in fact, Steven told me there were only three people, all men (Dansky, Knoebel, and Pitchford), in the Effeminist Movement. He then surprised me with his candor and honor as a man, and with his fairness as a gay historian: he apologized. His metanoia illustrated the forward maturation happening slowly in postmodern gay culture around the subject of S&M and homomasculinity.

8

LOUD GAY SILENCE
A MINI-BOOK REVIEW
LEATHER HISTORY ERASED IN *GAY L.A.*
A MODERNIST AUTHOR FRAMED IN A
POSTMODERN CULTURE

Larry's friend and *Drummer* editor, Jeanne Barney (1938-2019) wrote me her bitter opinion that her friend, Stuart Timmons (1957-2017), and his co-author Lillian Faderman, known as "the mother of lesbian history," reduced leather culture to four or five whispered asides in their 2006 book *Gay L.A.: A History of Sexual Outlaws, Power Politics, and Lipstick Lesbians*. Faderman was a professor at UCLA; and Timmons, the author of *The Trouble with Harry Hay*, had been mentored by *Advocate* editor and Radical Faerie Mark Thompson.

It pains me, a messenger not wanting to be beaten, to cite this exclusion which I mention only because Richard Fullmer predicted it and Larry suffered from it and Jeanne brought it up. This otherwise admirable book, which won two Lambda Literary Awards, seems a bit, well, fraudulent in its skirting of colorful LA "sexual outlaws" who wear leather. Was there not room in its 464 pages for one page about leather culture, politics, and activism? It does not mention the crusading Larry at all, and reductively flips off the heterosexual Jeanne (rhymes with "Queenie") with only three nods as the "straight woman" who edited *Drummer*.

Two years earlier, while Faderman's *Gay L.A.* manuscript was in production, was she reminded of Larry when her *Odd Girls and Twilight Lovers* and Larry's *The Leatherman's Handbook* were listed together in the Publishing Triangle's "100 Best Lesbian and Gay Novels"? Even though neither book is a novel.

Jeanne complained about the omissions on November 19, 2006, because Stuart had interviewed her for the book and had sent her a scan of his draft manuscript for input. In confirmation, John Embry had written to Jeanne on November 13, 2006, that at the ninetieth birthday party for Harry Hay's partner, John Burnside, that "Stuart Timmons...said you were most helpful with his new *Gay L.A.*"

On November 20, 2006, Jeanne wrote me an email titled "Gay—But Not Leather—LA":

> There are three (3) citations for me, one (1) each for John Embry and *Drummer*, and zero (0) for the Slave Auction, nor any mention of the Mark IV Baths. Stuart is one of those people who likes to pretend that he's "into leather." And Lillian is a Lesbyterian. On the other hand, however, there are two (2) citations for "Leather and Lace" and one (1) for the "Sado-Masochist Organization of Lesbians of Los Angeles," but zero (0) for the Leather Community; likewise for Larry.

While Jeanne's angry calculations were a bit off, Faderman and Timmons' à la carte servings of "LA history" dished up only passing mention of *Drummer* while ignoring the enormous gay-roots fact that it was a local magazine founded and filled in LA by local political activists, artists, and writers including local superstars like Larry and Jeanne. In 2010, Yale scholar Kate Kraft, advised by George Chauncey, noted Faderman and Timmons' failure to report on leather culture in the crucial eighth line of her thesis, *Los Angeles Gay Motorcycle Clubs, 1954-1980: Creating a Masculine Identity and Community.*

The LA authors snubbed the homomasculine magazine's cultural and gender-identity importance. They gave a cold shoulder to the hot scene of thousands of very real local "sexual outlaws"— as advertised in their book's bold subtitle—who were using *Drummer* and Larry's *Leatherman's Handbook* as their leather lifestyle bibles right there on location in LA. Was it systemic Marxism, feminism, separatism? Whatever it was, they canceled Larry Townsend. In their loud gay silence, the authors reduced the twenty-four-year history of *Drummer* to the one night the LAPD arrested forty-two leatherfolk at the famous Drummer Slave Auction on April 10, 1976—for which the LAPD has yet to apologize.

Distilling that event which was difficult history to vanilla folk, they invoked that night of injustice to make a cold point—not of specific empathy for leather culture, or for the victims targeted for being gay and arrested for being leather—but about the general anti-gay abuse systemic in the LAPD.

While creating the content of their book, they may have taken a tone from very vocal activists who, romancing Communism, rather typified the kind of far-left folk who drove Larry and average gay guys nuts with politically-correct agenda that twisted the reporting of gay history. One activist, who was a co-founder of the Gay Liberation Front in New York, and a member of the Trotsky-Communist Lavender and Red Union in Los Angeles, poked his head up and denounced the concept of the charitable Drummer Slave Auction as racially insensitive, which was a bit of a stretch, but was no reason for anyone to throw leather culture itself under the bus.

Why did the scholarship of these authors ignore not only Larry but also the local treasure-trove diary and gender archives of the vivid homomasculinity preserved in LA-born *Drummer*? Why not dig into a motherlode of 20,000 pages of gay history, customs, and desire written, drawn, and photographed mostly by the sexual-outlaw readers themselves during twenty-four years of 214 monthly issues from 1975-1999?

Because every author has every right to set parameters for a project, Faderman and Timmons must not be blamed for their choices or for Larry's mental state of reaction to them in 2006. But can you imagine how the veteran gay-elder Larry, age 76, who was such a famous and dominant and proven activist, author, and LA personality felt about this perceived cut? "Only in his home town, among his relatives and in his own house is a prophet without honor." (Folk wisdom in Mark 6:1-6) Through no fault of his own, while he was been born male, white, and privileged, he nevertheless grew up, as have so many gay men, traumatized by the relentless homophobia of straight society. Learning empathy from that suffering, he tried never to exploit his white-male privilege, and he never felt entitled to anything he did not earn or merit. Larry may have been one of those alpha people who speak straight from the shoulder and straight from the heart, but he never told anyone what to do. He never canceled anyone.

Not being included in *Gay L.A.* the same year Fred died, added gay insult to existential injury. He lost his cool. Excluded from a book composed by, he thought, a faux leatherman, and a distaff peer who came out in LA near the same time he did in the 1950s, was the last straw. He fumed, "This is the thanks I get?" Did academic radicals accidentally radicalize him more? The way he turned pain into pleasure in an S&M scene, he turned his widower's grief into an author's survivalist rage. Feeling shunned, he took his operatic *Götterdämmerung* fury out on friends who fled, but he never kicked the dog.

He felt dishonored and cornered, but what novelist doesn't like to twist a big surprise into his plot with a big fat climax? Distempered by his bad experiences with separatists, he figured if gay Marxist radicals—not meaning Timmons or the scholarly Faderman who is a better writer than he—have an appetite to destroy what they cannot change, he, the author of *Master of Masters*, could cook up a dish of instant creme of revenge served not cold but hot by terrorizing gay bookstores and a gay publisher with a dramatic lawsuit—if it was the last thing he ever did.

And it was.

In the way the Catholic Church dismisses homosexuality itself as a moral disorder, this sex-negativity erasure is typical of vanilla authors confused by the seemingly dark texture of the leather pop culture which is beyond the ken of their dainty moral order. Michel Foucault, that un-dainty S&M leather player who enjoyed fisting at the orgiastic Barracks and Slot baths on Folsom Street in San Francisco, might have given counsel to Timmons and Faderman in the line from his essay "Nietzsche, Genealogy, History": "The purpose of history is to make visible all those discontinuities that cross us."

Because of the seemingly purposed censorship and bias inherent in such academic exclusions, I fear for Larry what Richard Fullmer/Dirk Vanden warned, and what Larry himself pointed out: that male authors of gay pop-culture erotic literature will continue to be excluded or marginalized by critics and historians who otherwise exclude very little other alternative queer writing from their stated inclusivity which eclipses the light these leather authors brought to their thousands of readers who learned from them ways for masculine-identified gay men to live a gay life. The shunning of these authors is a self-inflicted wound on gay studies. The double standard is a double cross. Literotica is a valid genre that need not be segregated in quotation marks. If exclusion is transactional apartheid, inclusion is transformative sodality.

My email acquaintance Aristide Joseph Laurent (1941-2011), co-founder of *The Advocate*, who at the invitation of Jeanne Barney moved his "Astrologic" column from *The Advocate* to *Drummer* for a dozen issues, explained how the thankless *Advocate* ignored Jeanne who, as one of its founding columnists, worked four-times longer for the infant *Advocate* than she did for the infant *Drummer*. Aristide, at the blog of William A. Percy, III, testified how Jeanne (and for that matter Larry) was snubbed by *The Advocate* at its fortieth-anniversary party in 2007, just one year after the publication of *Gay L.A.*

> September 19, 2007. "Hobnobbing in West Hollywood." *The Advocate* celebrated its 40th birthday in West Hollywood last night. Being the last of the Big Four who started *The Advocate* back in 1967, I was invited to attend ... not by the latest powers that be but by my friend Stuart Timmons, acclaimed author of the tell-all tome *Gay L.A.*
>
> The Hollywood Cat Lady (aka Jeanne Barney) was similarly snubbed but invited by Stuart to attend as one of the remaining Founding Fathers/Mothers of the gay press movement. She snubbed back and refused to attend. You don't go, girl. For anyone old enough to remember, Jeanne B used to write the advice column, "Smoke From Jeannie's Lamp," for the old *Advocate*.

9

LARRY, RELIGIOUS ART, AND
SEX MAGIC BEHIND HAPTIC LITEROTICA
ONE-HANDED READING: EROTICA OR PORN?
BONDAGE ISN'T BONDAGE
UNTIL YOU WANT OUT

In the 1970s, Larry's commercial writing helped set up an evolving fusion of high and low art which fellow marketing genius Robert Mapplethorpe perfected in the 1980s. Historian Stephen Rutledge wrote in the *WOW Report* marking Robert's seventy-fourth birthday, November 3, 2020: "Mapplethorpe made art and porn the same thing. That is his greatest contribution to our culture."

In the same way, it is useful to the history of gay pulp fiction to remember that photography itself even in the Pop Art 1960s was not accepted as a proper establishment art until the mid-to-late 1970s when Mapplethorpe and his powerful and rich lover Sam Wagstaff began collecting antique photography, put high prices on it, linked Mapplethorpe's calculated homages to it, and declared to international dealers and critics that photography was indeed an art worthy of collectors, galleries, and museums—and, if they didn't think so, well, maybe they were not as avant garde as they thought they were. Larry, in the same way, was daring gay gatekeepers to accept S&M Literotica on its own terms. Or were they not as inclusive as they thought they were?

The purpose of Literotica is orgasm. The purpose of Literotica is sex that starts in the head and works its way down. Mapplethorpe told me in a letter that he liked "intelligent sex." Even more than writers of mainstream fiction working to suspend the disbelief of willing readers, erotic writers are hypnotists, magical creators casting their spelling with runes of the alphabet which the seduced reader sees in his mind's eye and makes haptic in his nonverbal hand. The *Sefer Yetsirah*, the mystical *Book of Creation*, dramatizes God manipulating the Hebrew alphabet to create the world. In the New Testament, the Word is made Flesh in the Body of the Christ. It takes a special talent to turn sex into literature, and literature into porn vivid enough to excite the reader's suspension of sexual disbelief. The money shot is the business of Literotica, and Larry made a small fortune from grateful readers he'd given a hand.

Erotica is aggressive and interactive. Having studied Catholic theology, ritual, and art for eleven years in a Vatican-run pontifical seminary (where no one ever molested me), may I suggest this parallel about the psychology of erotica. There exists a kind of invocative transubstantiation for eager readers of sex writing, much like a priest sets in motion in the Catholic Mass with his ritual words, "Hoc est enim corpus meum" meaning "This is my Body." Saying this, the priest changes the bread and wine in his hands into the Flesh and Blood of the Christ which he then lays on the tongues of cooperating believers willing to suspend disbelief in search of ecstatic Communion with the God-Man they worship.

The Crucifixion, because of Catholicism's deep stamp within art traditions, is a primary image and psychological hang-up in western art and culture. Muscular Christianity with its patriotic discipline of virility inspired without irony by the superhero stoicism of the fasting and tortured Christ demands boys "Man-Up for Jesus." Joris-Karl Huysmans acknowledged in his perfectly decadent book of fetishes, *Against Nature*, how viral was "the Church and her hereditary influence." More than one altar boy, when told during his adolescent magical mystical tour to be an "Imitation of Christ," has been transfigured from prayer to orgasm by the sadomasochistic sex appeal, and stamina, of the athletic Crucifixion sculpture, six-pack and all, of the multiple-choice handsome, bearded, bruised, bleeding bodybuilder Jesus Christ Superstar nailed up, naked but for a gossamer posing pouch, crowned with thorns, life-size and larger, looming over every Catholic altar like an Olympic gymnast poised in the "Iron

Cross" on the still rings. Religion has made a fortune selling erotic masochism based on the "Humiliation of the Christ."

Larry, who was not at all religious, picked up such an education on his grand tour of European churches and museums about this iconic connection, this desired hallucination, of Catholic imagery with S&M that he made special mention of the *Catholic Martyrology* as a "jewel" of a source book which drips with S&M details of the sexual martyrdom of voluptuous naked Christian youths tortured by uniformed Roman soldiers and leather-clad gladiators in the Colosseum.

> The first jewel [in my collection] came to me for one buck, through the Marboro Book catalogue. [Marboro mail-order was then the nation's largest retailer of remaindered books before it was bought up and consumed by Barnes & Noble.] It is entitled: *TORTURE* [his caps] *of the Christian Martyrs* (Illustrated), adapted by A. R. Alinson from the "DE SS. MARTYRM CRUCIATIBUS" [his caps] of the Rev. Father Antonio Gallonio. [Larry misnamed the book whose actual title is *De Sanctorum Martyrum Cruciatus*.]

The erotic author's collaborator is the one-handed reader with a prehensile grip and a prehensile mind. Invoking the gods Eros and Priapus, the author and reader become one in a physical connection that breaks existential isolation and spills seed. The reader's orgasm is the author's best review.

Literotica exists to arouse a super-willing suspension of disbelief in the reader who in the privacy of his mind uses masturbation as a dopamine ritual of magical thinking that leads to the self-care of physical pleasure and of existential visions of desire—like pop songs and opera that ignite musical thrills; like poetry inspiring mystical experiences. When masturbation isn't self-empowerment, you're just jerking yourself off. Orgasmic literature courts revelations of sexual identity. Orgasm doesn't lie. Tell me what you jerk off to and I'll tell you who you are.

Language has power words can't describe. About the impossibility of defining pornography, Justice Potter Stewart, in the most famous phrase ever uttered by the U.S. Supreme Court, said he couldn't define it, but "I know it when I see it." (Larry quoted Potter Stewart.) You either get the alchemy or you don't. Sex is personal. People can transubstantiate anything from bible stories to the *Sears Catalog* to NFL football telecasts into porn. In the alchemy of eros, if readers cum, it is their orgasm sorting the denotations and connotations of erotica and porn which, like beauty, are in the mind of the beholder. Erotica doesn't become porn until you cum—the way bondage isn't bondage until you want out.

Larry, who had no aspirations about pushing the margins of the canons of religion, art, and literature, knew how to rouse the sexuality of his readers. That's an art in itself. Not every author can or will do that. It's proverbial that the gay erotic writer is to gay non-erotic writers what Ginger Rogers was to Fred Astaire. Gay erotic literature can do everything gay mainstream literature can, but it does it backwards and in high heels adding to its Olympic degree of difficulty. Both porn and literary erotica can be fine art and pop art and lowbrow and highbrow and interchangeable.

Seventeen years after Michael Bronski in 1984 wrote a marvelous essay about male love in S&M novels titled "S/M: The New Romance" in Boston's *Gay Community News*, Vol, 2, No. 30, he wrote this 2001 call to arms in his essay, "Fictions about Pulp," in the *Gay and Lesbian Review*, 6, November 2001

> [These books] ...are an integral aspect of gay male culture and gay history that is as vital as—indeed inseparable from—our fight for legal equality and personal freedom. They are the records—albeit fictional ones, often seen through the peculiar lenses of their times—of how gay men lived, thought, desired, loved and survived.

Wayne R. Dynes, editor of the *Encyclopedia of Homosexuality*, led the charge toward scholarship in the "Duke University Guide to Pulps":

> Written primarily by gay men..., they served as primers on gay cultural norms for newly coming out or isolated gay men. At first, these gay-themed books did not

acknowledge the possibility of a "gay life," just "gay sex," but as gay culture and politics developed, gay fiction reflected a new all-encompassing culture separate from the straight world.

Drewey Wayne Gunn wrote in his *The Golden Age of Gay Fiction* that his younger self discovered the joys of gay pulp fiction when he found Larry Townsend's paperbacks in a local drugstore. He also discovered there was a genre of "Gay Science Fiction" with Larry's *2069*, and a genre of "Gay Mysteries" with Larry's *The Sexual Adventures of Sherlock Holmes* by "J. Watson" aka Larry.

With these critics and scholars, including Susan Stryker's book *Queer Pulp: Perverted Passions* (2001), their general acknowledgments include Larry in lists and sentences, but without development. That's a beginning. Larry Townsend, a writer, thinker, and psychologist who taught generations of leatherfolk how to live, was all of that, and he deserves specific study.

My own point of view is simply personal memoir in this my last testament about my relationship with Larry. His views are his views alone. I am but his friend spilling a drop for a lost brother. Because we bonded over writing, I cast about for literary comparisons. I am not F. Scott Fitzgerald's narrator Nick Carraway pining to make his pal James Gatz, who changed his name to "Jay Gatsby," stand at moral attention forever. Larry needs no one to explain him away.

If Larry's history is anything, it is a cautionary tale about gay men growing older and losing their cool the way Larry did and Truman Capote did and Quentin Crisp did and Tennessee Williams did and Gore Vidal did who "died of booze and revenge" according to his frenemy Edmund White. If Larry had paid attention to any one of them, he might have learned not to become the litigious gay old man yelling at the neighbors' kids to get off his gay lawn.

Larry and I had a fond fraternal regard for each other and for each other's boundaries. In the last thirty years, I have written about him, with his cooperation, in three books: his *Leatherman's Handbook*, Silver Anniversary Edition; *Gay San Francisco: Eyewitness Drummer*; and *Gay Pioneers*. His objective placement in history is yet to be written by more objective journalists, historians, and scholars who will come to appreciate the pleasure of his company once they realize his S&M books are not bound with human skin.

They have a lot of heavy lifting to do. As late in the gay enlightenment of the fin de siècle as October 26, 1995, the *Bay Area Reporter* allowed its so-identified trans-lesbian "Sapphistication" columnist to take a tasteless potshot at the elder Larry as the "...author of that classic of dead cow, *The Leatherman's Handbook*."

This memoir is banking an investment in future gay studies by disclosing private archival eyewitness documents and the local color around them. Perhaps a proper scholarship of reclamation history may begin to emerge to celebrate his hundredth birthday in 2030.

10

A 10-INCH POUND OF FLESH
WHEN THE LEGEND BECOMES FACT
THE CIVIL WAR OVER GENDER
"THE SOCIETY TO CUT UP MEN"

Hollywood director John Ford said, "When the legend becomes fact, print the legend." You know: like the history of the Stonewall riot. I'm not serving up any such media lie for the Legend Himself who, as a person and an author, delivered his truths about others to themselves in his books and advice columns. Realistically, Larry was a kind of Exhibit A of a homomasculine gay man traumatized twice: first by straight homophobes for not being a man, and second by politically-correct homosexists for being a man. He lived in anti-male times.

Just as he was entering publishing, he, and all of us back then, had to cope with the man-hating separatist Valerie Solanas who founded her "Society to Cut Up Men" and wrote her *SCUM Manifesto* published by Larry's rip-off publisher Maurice Girodias in 1967. That was the year before Solanas shot and wounded Andy Warhol and my dear friend, the British art critic and leatherman Mario Amaya, in Warhol's Factory on June 3, 1968. That was two days before a gunman mortally wounded presidential candidate Robert F. Kennedy on June 5 in the kitchen of the Ambassador Hotel in Los Angeles, eight miles from Larry's home where he sat writing *The Kiss of Leather*.

Making his own way, the trained psychologist worked on himself to re-shape his existential angst, and to correct his defensive gender anger, into political action and creative sadomasochism beloved by like-minded leathermen. He was one of them. They made him a best-selling author who helped them negotiate positive masculinity in a gay culture dominated by drag and effeminacy that have equal right to exist and compete but not to exclude. Male representation is not male domination. It is not gender tyranny. Homomasculinity, which is Walt Whitman's virile strength in *Leaves of Grass*, need not be erased by people who are afraid of men. Flagging existential rainbow reality, homomasculinity is nonaggressive, respectful, open, and equal in social justice to every other declarative queer identity. Homomasculinity aspires to represent the platonic ideal of the best that human males can be minus the toxic worst of racism, sexism, and ageism. As the coiner of the word *homomasculinity* in 1978 with first use in *Drummer* 31, September 1979, may I clarify that archetypal *homomasculinity* is never a synonym for stereotypical *hypermasculinity*. Toxic masculinity does indeed exist in some men and some women, but masculinity itself is natural and non-toxic.

In the separatist civil war over gender identity in the early 1970s, Larry Townsend was a political pamphleteer, who, like a gay Tom Paine, wrote many essays encouraging unity. The setting of one of Larry's first historical novels, *The Adventures of Captain Goose*, is the American Revolution. Long before the killjoy cancel-queer Richard Goldstein wrote his anti-leather screed, "S&M: The Dark Side of Gay Liberation," in *The Village Voice*, July 7, 1975—just two weeks after publication of the first issue of *Drummer*—Larry was writing common-sense theories about gay liberation, gay character, and police brutality in dozens of political columns in dozens of gay pop-culture publications such as *The Advocate*, *Vector*, *Drummer*, *Honcho*, *Entertainment West*, *California Scene* (published alongside Christopher Isherwood), *H.E.L.P. Incorporated Newsletter*, *Data-boy*, and *Coronet* (writing about himself as "Ralph Clark.") *Ralph* was the name of his nephew who for twenty-four years (1992-2016) owned the restaurant "Bistro Ralph" north of the Golden Gate Bridge in Sonoma County on the main square in Healdsburg where we often dined with Larry not far from our home.

The Advocate in a burst of pure pop-culture camp so liked his novel, *The Scorpius Equation*, it created a new gay cartoon strip based on it in 1972 called *Alpha and the Scorpions*. As an action-driven novelist, Larry also wrote activist journalism to rally leatherfolk to resist the intramural intra-minority, gay-versus-gay stressors, and sexism of the politically correct.

Literary arbiter, Winston Leyland, the former Catholic priest and founder of Gay Sunshine Press, who published three of my leather fiction books, wrote about Larry's novels in "Looking at Pornography" in proto-*Drummer* 1, 1971, saying judgmental gay liberationists

> usually take a "beneath contempt" approach to gay porno novels. If mentioned at all, they are usually airily dismissed with the usual [Marxist] cliches of "sexist capitalist exploitation"....The chief function of porno novels... is fantasy...solitary sex, and orgasm. Now the ideal presented by gay liberation is a situation where gay brothers and sisters are able to communicate verbally and sexually without...considerations of age, beauty, and other limitations ...Religious conservatives down through the centuries have barred sex outside established norms. How ironic it would be if we gay liberationists fell into a similar "holier than thou" syndrome.

Why do uptight gay heretics resisting the gay god Priapus think that three-dimensional character development in erotica is about no more than the protagonist's hardening 10-inch pound of flesh? In truth, many sex authors of gay men's adventure stories go way beyond their hero's endowment to write literary erotica with proper character development, plot, dialogue, style, and wit. Larry never won a Lambda Literary Award for his best-selling work, because Lambda, founded in 1989 did not consider erotic writing as a specific literary category until 2001 when he was 71 and past his prime. Reviewer Richard Labonté, the founder of A Different Light Bookstores, and the editor who included Larry in his *Best Gay Bondage Erotica* anthology, suggested in his November 23, 2010 email: "I think the first erotica award was implemented 2001, but maybe 2002."

In 1993 for the Fifth Lambda Literary Awards, Larry was nominated for his novel *Masters' Counterpoints*. The nod for the trophy was listed politely as a "Gay Mystery" because the category for racy "Men's Erotic Fiction" did not yet exist. This publishing contract between strange bedfellows happened because Larry, always the smartest marketing person in the room, fluffed up two of his older S&M murder novels, both featuring his detective Bruce MacLeod, and submitted them to the newly founded Alyson Press which was soliciting established authors to build its list of titles, including two of mine. Alyson, signing up his famous name, jumped to publish his *Masters' Counterpoints: A Bruce MacLeod Mystery* and his *One for the Master, One for the Fool: A Bruce MacLeod Mystery*.

Because Alyson was owned by that group that also owned *The Advocate*, Larry benefitted from the corporate synergy that boosted them, and promoted him, while he used them in his relentless lifelong marketing plan of selling his reprint rights for his old titles to new publishers designing new covers to reach new readers. The trap of his game plan caught him in the jots and tittles of legal contracts and copyrights with a variety of publishers from Alyson in Los Angeles to Modernismo and Masquerade Books in New York to Nazca Plains in Texas to Bruno Gmünder Verlag in Germany. Not all broke bad, but his tactics led to troubles that bedeviled his life, and to a scandal that hovered over his deathbed.

11

BLACKLISTS AND
GRUDGE MATCHES TO THE DEATH

By the nature of personality, Larry was a gay alpha male trapped inside a straight steak-and-bourbon body of a 1950s conservative right-wing Air-Force intelligence officer and Cold War veteran who disliked, he said, "subversives" infiltrating gay culture from the right and the left. In the political style of midcentury Republicans like Senator Joe McCarthy with his anti-gay House Un-American Activities Committee, and his sleazy gay attorney Roy Cohn, Larry kept a list of local gay political opponents, but, doing it defensively, he did them no aggressive harm unlike his frenemy, *Drummer* publisher John Embry, whose peevish blacklist insulted, exploited, and excluded talents like Robert Mapplethorpe, Tom of Finland, Fred Halsted, and frequent cover photographer Jim Wigler who all demanded proper bylines, copyright, and payment.

From time to time, Embry also blacklisted Larry and his own former *Drummer* editor Jeanne Barney whom he trashed virulently while I was editor in *Drummer* 30, June 1979—after which he blacklisted me for objecting to, among other things, his attack on her. I was still on his blacklist twenty-seven years later when he, who was not very tech-savvy, told Jeanne on November 13, 2006, that I was "stuffing Google" with my name and deleting his name because in his dog-eat-dog searches my name came up more than his. (I did not know I had such powers.) Embry, corporate president of his Alternate Publishing Inc, operated very like the dysfunctional Other Traveller and Olympia presses that exploited the talent.

Just as Jeanne was an intimate in the domesticity of Larry and Fred, she was privy to the domesticity of John Embry and Mario

Simon. In 2006, she painted a cosy, but lonely, picture recalling that John and Mario, life partners in publishing and real estate, enjoyed whiling away the hours sitting on the front porch of one of their homes at the Russian River—where they never invited Larry, so he said, on one of his frequent trips north—going over and over the blacklist of people they imagined had "done 'em wrong." Jeanne wrote on September 24, 2006: "Personally, being on that list is almost a source of pride, rather like being on Nixon's Enemies List." Embry once described himself sitting in a chair and threatening his rental tenants "like the Godfather, smiling and cracking his knuckles."

The grudge match between mail-order business competitors John and Larry began in 1972, and for all the publishing collaborations and the air-kiss brunches they shared in LA, it lasted till death. When Fred died in 2006, Embry wrote to Jeanne that she needn't "bother"—his word—sending Larry's address so he could mail Larry a sympathy card. Carrying his grudges, he said he did not recall hearing from Larry when his own lover, Mario Simon, died thirteen years earlier in 1993. And he sniped that when Larry and Fred came to San Francisco that Fred was the only one who would enter Embry's building because Larry, carrying his own grudges, stayed in the car. When Larry lay dying in Intensive Care, I wrote to Embry to let him know.

> From Jack Fritscher. To: John Embry, July 23, 2008. 3:33 PM. Subject: Larry Townsend in ICU. John, Our friend Larry Townsend is in ICU. Hopefully, he may rally, but the situation seems very distressed. If you want more info, please let me know. If you don't want to know, let me know. May our world of writers and readers keep Larry in our thoughts and give him good energy during the next few hours and days. —Jack Fritscher

> From: John Embry. To: Jack Fritscher. July 23, 2008. 6:02 PM. Subject: Re: Larry Townsend in ICU. [Embry writing in all UPPER CAPS] JACK, THANK YOU FOR NOTIFYING ME. ALTHOUGH LARRY'S AND MY RELATIONSHIP IS IN ABOUT THE SAME STATE

AS HIS AND JEANNIE'S [sic]. BE THAT AS IT MAY, I WISH HIM WELL AND WAS VERY DISMAYED AT FRED'S PASSING WHICH I AM SURE WAS VERY HARD ON HIM. —John Embry

12

THE CONSERVATIVE DILEMMA AND THE CONFUSING NAZI SUBTEXT OF LEATHER CULTURE "THE HIGH PRIEST OF S&M"

By the nurture of sexuality, Larry, because homosexuality is an inner teacher that guides us, changed most of his reactionary nature and disciplined himself to evolve to positive centrist values around race and gender diversity, and to exit the Republican Party. In the early 1970s, Larry converted, and became a leading gay activist Democrat because it was the right thing to do in the gay mainstream when the principal debate in the gay lib of the 1970s was, as preached in *The Advocate*, about what kind of respectable gays in suits and ties, rather than bohemians in beads, or freaks in leather, should represent us in American media and popular culture.

After the 1971 Christopher Street Pride Parade in West Hollywood, the Republican Larry wrote an editorial against people wearing suggestive pop-art costumes. He recoiled from future Academy Award Oscar Streaker and leatherman Robert Opel marching inside his seven-foot-tall "Mr. Penis" costume, and from a guy dressed up as a life-size jar of Vaseline. He specifically denounced a "Cockapillar" costume created by gay crusader Pat Rocco (1934-2018) who began directing gay films he sold via mail-order in 1968 at the same time that Larry began writing gay novels. Like Townsend and Opel, Rocco became a frequent contributor to *Drummer*. His "Cockapillar" construction was a giant pink bulldozer penis head fronting a long horizontal matching cock-shaft worn on the backs of seven performance artists walking a conga-line of legs through the crowds much like a dragon in a Chinese New Year parade. Faced with this irresistible market trend of gay pop culture toward deploying ever more outrageous performance-art drag, he changed his tune.

Larry was typical of many queer folk who, born into conservative families, would otherwise grow up as fundamentalist as their parents—except for that wild card of homosexuality which offers them a way out of the sins of the parents, and schools them into empathy, and often, in this metanoia, turns them liberal if their personality is more balanced than it is just plain "Iowa Stubborn." Sometimes, on the sliding scale of politics, some, born into right-wing Christian families, turn coat, but not temperament, and become far-left reactionaries. He was so personally aware of this fundamentalist struggle that he addressed the issue directly in "The Conservative Dilemma," Chapter 14 in *Leatherman's Handbook II*.

In *The Advocate*, May 23, 1973, Martin St. John reported on left-wing extremists, costume issues, and the attempt to de-gay the LA gay parade:

> In 1972, the [gay] parade planning was taken over, by and large, by militant gay women—one group sworn to "clean up" [the costumes worn in] the parade, the other agitating for an anti-war, rather than a gay pride, theme, for the march.

Larry exited the macho right-wing of his military youth, and marched to the viable political center. The trained spy warned that the gay left-wing was as unsustainable as the right, despite the fantasy that all the best gay folk are leftist and wonderful just because in the gay-lib ponzi pyramid so many early organizers visible in the news media were left-wing activists and Communists like Mattachine founder Harry Hay who helped originate gay political resistance in the 1940s and 1950s.

Larry, a psychologist graduated from UCLA and trained by the Air Force in gathering military intelligence, watched the Hollywood *mise en scene* of gay revolution in Silver Lake turn the aspirational Mattachine Steps into a gay Odessa Steps sequence of queer mutiny. He was an observant witness and critic who reacted to the right-left polarity, cannibal infighting, and Communism inside the LA Mattachine Society itself in 1953 when red-baiting conservative and progressive power struggles famously caused the entire Mattachine board of founders to take opposing sides and resign in a mid-1950s act of gay separatism that inflamed the gay civil war in which Larry soon served.

Larry, the anti-Communist, was not fascist or Nazi. In fact, he was a leader of organized resistance against gay and straight authoritarian diktats. He loomed large in Los Angeles media when S&M was not understood in gay pop culture. At the moment he founded his LT Publications, he was attacked by some for being the ringleader stoking the rise of fascism in gay culture because S&M seemed much too authoritarian to gay-libbers who thought that S&M in the bedroom caused fascism in the streets. In the *Los Angeles Free Press*, April 14, 1972, Craig A. Hanson, the founder emeritus of the Los Angeles Gay Community Alliance, exposed his own bias.

> Fundamentally, S&M is authoritarian, demanding superior-inferior relationships, and, as I have a disturbing suspicion [shared by the politically-correct extremists and the LAPD], a penchant for an authoritarian society.

Leathermen über alles? Isn't that the silly heart of Mel Brooks' satirical 1967 Academy Award winner, *The Producers*?

Hanson headlined his *J'Accuse* anti-S&M feature with the snarky gender-snap title, "Locked Up by Closet Queens: Gay Sadomasochism." He identified Larry as an S&M "High Priest," and denounced him as the *cause* of all the trouble in River City.

> As my article explains, I do not approve of the S&M Cult or of sadomasochism, but it exists and needs explaining...because of the election of S&M "High Priest" Larry Townsend as president of H.E.L.P. (Homophile Effort for Legal Protection).

Reacting to Larry and his homomasculine leather fans, Hanson continued, revealing the rise in the civil war of gay Quislings threatening and terrorizing other gays.

> ...a new and very secret organization, Gay Zap, has been... sending crank letters to S&M bars...demanding changes of policy...and promising police action against the S&M people if they don't change their politics and behavior.

Then like a Nielsen Rating of trends in gay pop culture, he wrote he was concerned by the

> ...rise in the S&M personal ads [attracted by Larry's columns] in *The Advocate* newspaper so they now account for 20% of the listings...

In a grudging compliment, he noted all the new and welcome "political activity by the seventeen Los Angeles bike and leather-oriented clubs and the nine leather-western gay bars." Then he had to admit something about the undeniable value of Larry's political action that Larry began at H.E.L.P.

> This [leather] subculture is a very stable element in the gay community (many bike clubs have been going for years) and constitutes its greatest organizational reservoir.... Only recently [along with Larry] have they shown an interest in gay civil rights.

He closed defining the anti-leather bigotry that Larry as a Leather Sisyphus was up against.

> For many, gay and straight alike, no other form of sexual expression seems more repulsive than sadomasochism.... Gay liberation is not just for counter-culture gays and political radicals because they say they have the proper political or social consciousness, nor is it only for transvestites and other fem-identified males just because they have flung their homosexuality in the face of society for so long. There can be no second-class gay people who must remain in the closet while the rest are liberated. By ignoring and even persecuting S&M people, organized homosexuality—the gay newspapers, churches, political groups, and liberation organizations—has done exactly what straight society has done to the rest of us.

Calling for understanding, Hanson called for action.

> Homosexual sadomasochism is one subject the gay liberation movement has never discussed....S&M has been the bad boy of the gay world, and only during the past months has anything been written about it....Coming to terms with S&M is one of the real challenges for the gay lib movement.

Even so, he could not help confusing sex and violence about leather fun and games in Hollywood where costumes and role-playing ought to be understood.

> S&M...supposedly directs violence by channeling it to certain specific sexual encounters. Men are drawn from those sublimated homosexual desires which [here, amazingly, he condemns male homosexuality itself with a blood libel] have boiled over into war, and into violence eroticized into sex. Ever read about the origins of the Nazi Party? Most of the early Nazis were homosexual sadomasochists, and they didn't sublimate anything.

With malice like that, no wonder that Larry from the first time he put pen to paper spent his long vocation as a goodwill ambassador writing men's S&M adventure stories in handbooks, novels, stories, and advice columns to educate readers about the existential truth and value of leather culture.

It's gay gossip that some people from liberal to conservative on the Rainbow Spectrum—acting, or reacting, out of identity politics or existential curiosity or empathy or counterphobia—are sometimes driven by a sweet lust to put their intellectual, political, racial, and gendered ideas of their public selves aside to seek out their own literal physical experiences in top or bottom S&M role-play in private scenes in imaginary military brigs, southern plantations, and concentration camps. If they don't dare play in a real dungeon with a real sex partner, they do it solo masturbating to the pop culture of books, magazines, and videos in the multibillion-dollar kink sex industry.

Most people are bottoms most of the time, and consumers are voracious for magazines like *Drummer* and books like Larry's which led the Stonewall Era charge into kink fantasy. Through the years, I've worked with the subscription lists of several gay magazines and video companies which contain the names of famous folk who live politically-correct vanilla lives by day, but keep S&M art, literature, and porn under the bed where their friends can't see their guilty pleasure and hypocrisy. Larry's lists were just the same. They thrive on this conflation which socially rejects the very leathersex that sexually defines their passion. Their framed print of the Mapplethorpe calla lily hanging in the dining room gets a secret *frisson* from the Mapplethorpe cock hanging in the bedroom.

It is a gay popular-culture truth: millions more people read the 214 issues of *Drummer*, with its monthly press run of 42,000 copies at its height during twenty-four years (1975-1999) than have read all that fin de siècle's best-selling American gay novels combined. A book comes out sealed with its author's ideas once. A magazine comes out refreshed with its contributors' new ideas monthly.

There is many a man in leather, and many a member of the gay uniform clubs, and many a Leni Riefenstahl film fan whose erotic imagination trumps absolute political correctness. At more than one leather bar on its midweek movie night, such as Larry's San Francisco favorite, the Ramrod, the bartender often screened a twenty-minute montage of beautiful homoerotic images of male athletes, including Black gold-medalist Jesse Owens, from the 1936 Berlin Summer Olympics. The clip was cut, minus its Nazi propaganda, from Riefenstahl's film, *Olympia* (1938). If 1970s leathermen had been actual Nazi sympathizers, they'd have been watching Riefenstahl's *Triumph of the Will* (1935).

We men who flourished in the 1970s are the last gay generation alive to remember the winds of that war. Larry and I and boys like us lived through those five terrifying years playing "soldier" shooting at Nazis and dropping rocks off the roof of the garage yelling, "Tojo! Tojo! Bombs over Tokyo!" Tom of Finland, at our first meeting on February 9, 1978, told me how much erotic impact Nazi men had on him. Tom was twenty-five when the war ended and Larry was fifteen and I was six. Tom's compeer, the edgier artist Rex, born during the war, was, because of his coded fine-art portfolios of severe Teutonic-American leathermen, denounced as a "Naziphile" in that ad absurdum essay, "S&M: The Dark Side of Gay Liberation" in *The Village Voice*, July 7, 1975. In response in 1976, *Drummer* published a Rex leatherman stylishly harnessed on the cover of the "Holiday Issue," number ten; and then featured the pointillist artist alongside Robert Mapplethorpe (who collected Rex's prints and was influenced by Rex's leather visions) in the 1978 special S&M art issue, *Son of Drummer*.

Many S&M men, especially those born around the midcentury World War, fantasize about fascism in the same way that Larry, who served as a teenage anti-Nazi plane-spotter at the Peddie School, romanced fascism by transposing its evil power plays—in the counterphobic way leather culture digests problematic realities—into the beating sadomasochistic heart of his writing. Larry was a purposeful reader gleaning world history whose undercurrents of sex and sadism he adapted into dozens of sexy historical novels from *The Fairy King: The Life of Henri II, King of France* (1970) to his 649-page magnum opus, *Czar! A Novel of Ivan the Terrible* (1998). As shown in photos, a shelf in his office was lined with several best-selling histories of the Third Reich. When stationed with the U.S. Air Force in Germany, he became a devotee of Joseph Musil's bildungsroman *Young Törless*, a 1906 novel he recommended about S&M brutality in the German military just before the rise of the Nazis. Larry, the political activist, was so aware of the pop-culture confusion of leather and Nazis that he directly addressed the psycho-erotic nexus with many references throughout both *The Leatherman's Handbook* and its sequel *The Leatherman's Handbook II* (1983) in which he wrote:

> I can't imagine anyone in his right mind seriously wanting to revert to this [Nazi] period. As with many other historical evils, the fantasy will exclude the reality and the horror. We focus only on the parts we find stimulating, or titillating. The same barrier of time and/or space makes it possible to look on other atrocities in a very different light from the people who had to endure them:

Nazi Germany, Vietnam, Czarist Russia, Inquisitionist Spain, Borgian Italy, various Latin American settings. Such are often the bases for many of our best and most exciting stories.

After every war, with or without Nazis, there is an afterglow of romantic and erotic nostalgia in popular culture, fiction, and films. In 1974 and 1975, while the next war in Vietnam was raging to its disgraceful end on the roof of the American Embassy, the first issues of *Drummer* went to press with a few images of actors in the previous war playing Nazis in Hollywood films. At that moment, movie critics could not decide if two ravishing hit films directed by women about sadomasochistic sex in concentration camps—Liliana Cavani's *The Night Porter* and Lina Wertmüller's *Seven Beauties*—were arthouse cinema or Holocaust porn.

In the 1970s of Larry's advent, every American gay-bar customer aged thirty and older had lived through the war with the Nazis. Our dear friend Hank Diethelm (1928-1983), the German immigrant owner of the popular Brig bar on Folsom Street in San Francisco, had been forced into the Hitler Youth, and at age seventeen in 1945 fled west to be rescued by American soldiers. He could never shake off his counterphobic lust for domination by perfect young Nazis. I could only imagine what private concentration camp fantasies went on in his head when in May 1970, he pitched me about filming a ritual castration scene of the kind Larry would write about in Chapter 9, "The Castration Complex, Real and Symbolic," in his second *Handbook*.

Knowing Hank, I figured he wanted to step out of himself and watch himself on screen in a kind of crypto-Nazi horror film, like Larry's favorite flick, Kenneth Anger's 1963 *Scorpio Rising*, starring himself in a Super-8 S&M scene. Often screened in leather bars including Hank's Brig, Anger's 28-minute film about gay-specific Nazi bikers had more influence shaping the twisting helix of the leather psyche than did Marlon Brando's straight film, *The Wild One* (1953).

Hank was a sweet man always aglow with *Gemütlichkeit* that got him whatever he wanted. So, because my then-lover David Sparrow and I were his house guests, we felt obliged to shoot the ten-minute bespoke film as a faked fantasia staged, with David as his co-star, in his basement dungeon on Bemis Street, but with absolutely no suggestion of anything Nazi because since my terrified wartime boyhood I've been anti-Nazi. In *Drummer* 128, assistant editor Ken Lackey confirmed my stance telling readers: "I'll bet Jack could lick ten neo-fascists with one hand tied behind his back!" So, regarding Hank's fetish, fourteen years of S&M play later in 1984, some people became further confused about S&M and Nazis when Hank was tied up and murdered and set on fire in the basement of his home by a leatherman who was likely mentally ill before he entered leather culture.

Like Hank, many a gay movie-goer of Larry's generation was amused in the 1970s by hilariously camp Nazisploitation films like the great Don Edmunds' *Ilsa: She-Wolf of the SS*, and *Salon Kitty* directed by Tinto Brass who also directed the wildly scandalous male-male "fisting film" *Caligula*, scripted by Gore Vidal and starring Helen Mirren; by Pier Paolo Pasolini's *Salo* which I reviewed aggressively in *Drummer*; and by films depicting Nazi General Ernst Röhm, the commander of the gay SA Brownshirt soldiers murdered during their exquisite orgy in deshabille drag on the "Night of the Long Knives" which Luchino Visconti dramatized operatically as thwarted gay romance in his 1969 film *The Damned*. Clips from the divine decadence of that motion picture, along with clips from Roger Corman's campy S&M flick *De Sade* (1969), were also frequently screened on Tuesdays, the typical movie night invented to drum up midweek business in leather bars.

Wised up to Nazis, the human condition, and the problem of evil, director Cavani, like Pasolini and Townsend, considered the works of de Sade as the basic text of human nature. She said de Sade should be taught in schools. Larry taught de Sade in his writing. Leather bars taught de Sade in their nightly tutorials. Leathermen did their homework.

Hitler's politically-correct Nazi party founded at the Furstenfelder Hof pub in Munich on January 5, 1919, was indeed centered around beer halls, homosexuals, camaraderie, uniforms, and short leather pants—just like gay leather culture.

No wonder that leathermen, crowding into darkened bars for those Tuesday movie nights, found an ironic outlaw *frisson* in standing en masse drinking, smoking, groping, and laughing at clips like "Springtime for Hitler," from *The Producers*.

Is there a movie-going leatherman alive who has not swooned in guilty pleasure to the platonic ideal of the stunning blond Hitler youth in Brownshirt uniform singing the fictitious fascist anthem, "Tomorrow Belongs to Me," in *Cabaret*? The gay and Jewish composers John Kander and Fred Ebb wrote the song to teach how seductive propaganda music can be. The song is so seductively uplifting that theater audiences were surprised and shocked at their own mixed emotions trying to resist the recruiting of its sunny hotsy-totsy Nazi sex appeal. Director Bob Fosse's *Cabaret* premiered in 1972 at the same moment Larry's *Handbook* was published.

Larry noted the undercurrent of comedy in S&M culture in his *Handbook II*:

> Even those long horsehide coats we see in vintage movies of the Nazi era can be quite a turn-on. I remember one night in a San Francisco bar [the Ramrod], watching a little guy in one of these Wehrmacht coats wandering around, and I was quite attracted to him until I got up close, and he whispered: "I vould lek to schpink you."

Publisher John Embry printed monthly display ads for the Gay Nazi Party in *Drummer* until I told him I'd quit as editor if he did not cease and desist. Larry in LA backed me in confronting Embry in San Francisco because, even though Larry was a West Hollywood action figure famous for whipping willing men to a Wagnerian beat, he was no fascist. He hated and equated Nazis, Communists, Marxists, and politically-correct gay extremists. Although he leaned conservative as alpha males often do, for all his bluster, you couldn't find real fascism, sexism, or racism in him with a Geiger Counter. It's all about perspective. (Six inches is what you make it.) What was ordinary fun for leathermen seemed extraordinary to outsiders. It is worth remembering that every avant-garde sex trip debuting in the new post-Stonewall trip of the Titanic 1970s—especially to leathermen during the 1970s—seemed like a huge exaggeration of reality that was, nevertheless, reality. And freedom. And fun.

As late as *Drummer* 115 (April 1988), publisher Anthony DeBlase, who bought *Drummer* from Embry, continued Mel Brooks' anti-Nazi camp when he published a full-page ad picturing a uniformed German with riding crop and tall boots disciplining a floored *Drummer* reader. Soliciting subscriptions, the tag line read with the stereotyped comedy accent, "You Vill [*sic*] Read *Drummer!*"

In the *H.E.L.P.Drummer Newsletter*, volume 2, number 6, March, 1973, Larry warned against the rising gay militias of the extreme right and the extreme left, revealing his particular concerns about the infection of political correctness among young men and women being brainwashed by the kind of male and female Marxist separatists whom he loathed for their exclusionary heresies, sexist politics, and penis envy that often made his blood pressure boil. He wrote:

> One of the most clear-cut indications that any social movement has "arrived" is the attempt by forces of the extreme right or extreme left to take it over. By this criterion, today's Gay Movement certainly qualifies.... A couple of weeks ago, the Kingmasters [men's group] were surprised to receive a visit by a gentleman who claimed to be "the American Party candidate for Governor in 1974."...In the question-and-answer period, the truth came out. This was the same man who had been placing classified ads in *The Advocate*, soliciting members for the "Gay Nazi Party."...The speaker was thanked and asked to leave.
>
> Unfortunately, not all of the usurpers are this transparent. With the fall of Nazi Germany and the demise of [Republican Senator] Joe McCarthy, the nuts on the right have been deprived of their major power bases. They are not to be discounted, but the seriousness of their threat cannot compare to the insidious potential from the other extreme. *The leftists have always been there,*

of course, but it has been quite awhile since we have seen them in all their malicious glory [Italics added]. Over the weekend of February 3rd, at the California Committee for Sexual Law Reform Convention (H.E.L.P. Center), the rock was lifted and out they came! Following the time-honored tactic of the Socialist Workers' Party, their unspoken battle cry was: *"Take it over if you can, and if you can't—Destroy it!"* [Italics his]

Sadly enough, as is typical in any of these Communist Front efforts, the ringleaders are the only ones who fully understand what they are doing. They assume the posture of gurus, wise men (or women), having indoctrinated a noisy, enthusiastic bevy of young followers with the carefully calculated party line. The kids who carry the ball are acting largely in good faith, unaware of the use being made of them. And so it was at the California Committee Convention.

The SWP [Socialist Workers Party] has made stronger and heavier inroads into the lesbian branch of the Movement than many of us suspected, while some of the men...were the old-time socialist revolutionaries we have seen and heard since the days of the *Gay Liberation Front* [Italics added].

Is this where it's at? I was under the impression that the Gay Movement had matured....that the rational approach of utilizing the laws and courts and the other mechanisms of the Establishment to gain our ends within the system was the route we were going to follow. Apparently, I was wrong.

Years later, in *The Leatherman's Handbook II*, he penned a special "negotiation" section titled "Women" in Chapter 14, "The Maestro's Circular File."

13

LUNCHING WITH LARRY: HANGED, DRAWN, AND (FRENCH) QUARTERED IN WEST HOLLYWOOD LAY IT AS IT PLAYS

You haven't experienced *echt* Los Angeles if you haven't entered a restaurant entourage with a star like Larry Townsend who knew how to make an entrance while ignoring the attention. Larry may not have been a giant of American literature, but he was a giant of a man. In his 1972 *Handbook*, he says he's a barefoot six-foot-one and 190 pounds. By 1985, the author in boots, coming in at six-foot-three and 240 pounds, was an inch taller than drag actor Divine at 300 pounds, and two inches shorter than Rock Hudson at 215 pounds. His natural air of superiority appealed to his readers in search of a master. He was an alpha male who was always head of the table and driver of the car. I never knew anyone who took so many people to brunch or to supper. Intent on keeping connected in gay LA, he and Fred were sociable members of a group of gents who regularly dined together at a variety of restaurants. From his Air Force training, he had the military command presence of a big cop in his height and build and aura. He was a larger-than-life character who not only loved opera, he *was* opera. Even so, in terms of sustainment, without Fred Yerkes, there would have been no Larry Townsend.

Hollywood is a strange country where appearance is reality that feeds the dreams and fantasies of the gay soul like no other city. Even before Joan Didion, who also started as a self-help columnist, captured its salacious straight and gay characters in her 1970 social-disaster novel *Play It as It Lays*, Larry's characters were selling their souls in his 1969 novel *The Faustus Contract*. He was a keen observer of his own gay LA, and a great tour director who like many an American male felt most free to talk while gripping a steering wheel. I loved the dark starry nights in Los Angeles when the docent Larry would drive Fred and Mark and me to supper to show off their favorite restaurants, and then drive us the long way home.

They were welcome "old faces" at the steak-and-lobster Café D'etoile, favored by Anne and Christopher Rice, where we sat jammed shoulder to shoulder in its close French café style seating with well-heeled, large, carnivorous gay men at 8941 Santa Monica Boulevard. They liked Mark's with its American-nouvelle cuisine spun out to tables by cheeky waiters at 861 N. La Cienega Boulevard, and Chez Jay, the steak-and-seafood beach-bar dive at 1657 Ocean Avenue in Santa Monica where Larry had been a regular since just after its founding in 1959, and they knew his name.

Those nights of "fine dining" were tea parties compared to Larry's years of long brunches at the French Quarter coffee shop which opened in 1973 inside the French Market at 7985 Santa Monica Boulevard, and closed in 2015. It was there in LA where all the world's a soundstage that the vicious circle around Larry held court they could never resist as frenemies because attitude and strife and co-dependency defined them and they could not quit each other.

Larry's cast of sitcom regulars for thirty-five years was the quartet of Barney, Embry, Legrand, and Earl, with guest-appearances by Larry's Fred, and by Embry's first and second sequential mates. Because of LAPD persecution, everyone in the core group had an arrest record.

As a member of the revolving audiences invited to their table, I could write fiction playing them as five characters in search of an author. Having collaborated separately with each one of them on several major projects on page and screen, including Mark and me shooting six S&M films with Earl and Legrand on location in Europe in 1989, I liked them, their experience, and their stories. Roger Earl, for instance, was for years the dresser at NBC-Television in Burbank for the singer Dean Martin from whom Earl borrowed ten-thousand dollars to bankroll—unbeknownst to Martin—the 1975 filming of the Earl-Legrand leather epic, *Born to Raise Hell*. Working with Martin in Las Vegas, Earl managed to make a nemesis out of Dean's co-star, Liza Minnelli. Larry should have been the group's ideal autobiographer, but he wasn't top enough to do it, and they weren't bottom enough to let him.

His first personal revelations, tied to the pre-publication of his first *Leatherman's Handbook*, appeared in his interview, "Larry Townsend Talks about His Life as a Gay Novelist," in *Vector*, October 1971. When the East Coast Eulenspiegel Society founded in 1971 approached the West Coast writer in 1974, he sent that seminal S&M group his personal essay "The Compatibility of Contrast" for its *Pro-Me-Thee-Us Newsletter*, No. 3, in which he explained his autobiographical timeline in helping establish the culture of defensive leather politics in Los Angeles. In 1983, he wrote a resume of his career in his "Introduction" to *The Leatherman's Handbook II*. Years later, he owned up that his book *Leather Ad-M*, and not *Leather AD-S*, was mostly autobiographical.

However, even casting about for literary equivalents in order to peg them, like the Algonquin Club, which they were not, might gloss over the original historical contributions of these talented folk who created at least three gay classics of transforming energy during a sexual revolution of radical change: Larry's *Leatherman's Handbook* (1972), Roger Earl and Terry Legrand's ground-breaking S&M film *Born to Raise Hell* (1974), and John Embry and Jeanne Barney's magazine *Drummer* (1975). They were serious, ordinary looking, older-generation people, mostly within ten years senior to me who listened to their small talk of mutual self-absorption that was fascinating until it became exhausting.

Thinking always of how to create desk jobs for themselves and how to cash in on the new leather culture, they skipped past the divine opportunities for sex at the height of the 1970s sexual revolution and chose to schmooze in safe bars and emcee leather-bar beauty contests. The men played at light S&M games enhanced by alcohol. They were not heavy players having mad passionate love affairs and out-of-the-body drug experiences in the rough-and-tumble classrooms of licentious bars, sex-club orgies, and risky street cruising—where authentic underground leathersex and art spontaneously combusted the way that street fashion often inspires haute couture. Unlike the leather poet Thom Gunn who lived the leather high life and went stoned to bars and baths and orgies to turn sex into literature in *My Sad Captains* and *The Man with Night Sweats*, they were not really S&M players personally involved with their leather topics. In 1973, *The Advocate* reported in "S&M: A Weekend Game":

> S&M is "a game to be played on the weekend," according to Larry Townsend, one of the best-known writers on the gay "leather" scene. Townsend, who has a Master's Degree in psychology, and has worked as a counselor and specialist in personnel motivation, *denies that he is deeply involved himself in S&M practices* [Italics added].
>
> He has, however, written a number of books and other publications on S&M in which he speaks with the authority of seemingly detailed knowledge and displays an extensive command of history.

Jeanne's dive into this leathersex scene was social and political and gendered. She stroked its art, entertainment, and public relations. The Robert Opel photograph of herself that she published in *Drummer* pictured her with Goldie Glitters of the Cockettes, illustrating Opel's cover feature on the Cycle Sluts, a genderfuck group of bearded men in *Rocky Horror Show* leather-and-lace drag who were kin in Los Angeles to the Cockettes in San Francisco. Jeanne even put the Sluts on the cover of issue 9 to the distress of male-identified subscribers complaining about, in terms of today's cancel culture, genderfuck queens occupying a male sanctuary magazine.

It did not help that the group took its name from Barbara Streisand who was not everyone's diva. Camping in black-vinyl boots and chaps with plastic chains, she starred in a three-way porn film titled *Cycle Sluts* inside her 1970 movie, *The Owl and the Pussycat*. On movie nights in leather bars, it was one thing to laugh at clips from that film, but it was another to find leather satire, suitable for a put-down in *Blueboy*, creeping into the only existing gay men's adventure magazine. It was not sexism. Subscribers did not complain when the evolving *Drummer* finally felt secure enough to introduce two women, the leather pioneers Cynthia Slater and Pat Califia, in my "Society of Janus" feature in *Drummer* 27, February 1979. By comparison, *The Advocate*, the magazine for affluent white males worshiping divas, did not add the word *lesbian* to its masthead until 1990.

Jeanne's miscalculation, disrupting the very leather homo-masculinity that sheltered her under its wing, unseated her authenticity with readers. Two issues later, it wasn't cause and effect exactly, but she quit as editor under cover of John Embry moving LA *Drummer* north to San Francisco. She, who was basically an advice columnist like Larry, lost what influence she had in *Drummer* where she was never again welcome. And from which she withdrew. Like Nathaniel West's fictional advice columnist, Miss Lonelyhearts, did she internalize the infectious problems of her readers which caused Miss Lonelyheart's depression, alchoholism, and infighting?

Larry genuinely liked holding court in sociable leather bars where his fans found him open and charming. No devotee of drugs, he often told his cautionary tale of how he—a chocoholic—once got so stoned in San Francisco on brownies he did not know were from a recipe by Alice B. Toklas, that after he left the dinner party to go to do "sex research" at the Glory Hole venue at 225 Sixth Street, he had to lock himself into one of the many blowjob cubicles the size of a small phone booth till the world stopped spinning. Frankly, if anyone ever needed a hit of acid to evolve himself, it was Larry Townsend. Concerning altering his mind, he wrote in Chapter 17, "The Social World of Leather," that he preferred San Francisco leather bars where they served liquor "while all the leather bars in Los Angeles get by on beer licenses."

Priding himself on keeping control with his limit of two alcoholic drinks, he preferred to play privately at home, boosting the scene with a modicum of poppers for the slave as he wrote in Chapter 9, "Booze and Drugs," in his first *Handbook*, and in Chapter 13, "Drugs, Booze, and Health," in his pre-AIDS *Leatherman's Handbook II*.

> Moderation in all things...Of the lot [alcohol and drugs], I am most comfortable using and having my partner use alcohol. In great excess it can have a debilitating effect. In lesser quantities, it can serve the greatest range of needs....Marines [during Vietnam, 1961-1975] being by far my favorite choice...I found...it frequently took a little time, a little talk, and a little booze to bring out the best in them...I tried to hit the area around the USO just about the time it closed on a Friday or Saturday night.

At the French Quarter, the group's glamour status was driving their flashy cars into its parking lot. Larry had his Corvettes and his luxury vans. Jeanne tooled around LA in her hot yellow Pontiac Solstice sports convertible. They drove the streets and wandered the freeways like characters Didion updated in *Play It as It Lays* with her magical thinking out of F. Scott Fitzgerald's *The Great Gatsby*, a novel she returned to again and again. Rarely entertaining each other at their homes, their custom was to drive to the neutral ground of the French Quarter where their exhibition matches were so much more fun than bickering over drinks in a private home. Each was a person of value. Each had a story of survival. But together were they bad for each other? The author, the editor, the publisher, the film director, the movie producer? Did Fitzgerald know their type? Did he foreshadow them in his x-ray novel of people trapped in their own privilege?

> They were careless people, Tom and Daisy—they smashed up things and creatures and then retreated back into their money or their vast carelessness or whatever it was that kept them together, and let other people clean up the mess they had made.

In this tale about the rise and fall of a specific gay generation, these experts at domination and submission were into everything with each other except sex and surrender. They played "Musical Chairs" with their enmities, and when the music stopped they were all left standing holding the bag of quarrels and isolation that marked their final years, and caused them all to die estranged from each other.

When poet Ian Young reviewed Larry's Hollywood novel, *Stalked*, in 1999, he transferred to Larry the Yeatsian keyword *slouch* that Joan Didion had relocated to LA in her *Slouching Towards Bethlehem*. He revealed a glimpse of how Larry's true blood ran in the rough bestiary of his Hollywood life, his friends, and frenemies.

> The story is about Ryan Franklin, a young Hollywood actor who gets stalked by a...drifter called Glen Leach. When Glenn slouches into Ryan's pampered Hollywood lifestyle, things get very ugly....There is not a single likeable character; everyone is selfish, jaded, amoral, and sexually driven.

The French Quarter was a gay space with a New Orleans Dixieland theme. It functioned as a lobby and dining room for the virtual Grand Hotel that was West Hollywood pop culture on permanent Mardi Gras parade. It was camp. It was touristy. It was local. It was like a dinner-theater set for a musical-comedy version of *A Streetcar Named Desire*. It was perfect. It was the place to see and be seen. It was where they plugged in. It made them feel visible, younger, still in fashion, and, sometimes, grand. No place in LA symbolized them singly and as a group more than this habitat, the chosen public environment of their endangered species.

And talk about the queer roots of WEHO at the French Quarter! For thirty-five years, I have subscribed to the show-biz bible, weekly *Variety*, and have been given some vintage issues by friends. In 1933, toward the finale of the 1920s Pansy Craze, *Variety* reported on this one-mile unincorporated county strip of Santa Monica Boulevard stretching several blocks between what became the French Quarter, and what was then United Artists Studio at the corner of Santa Monica and Formosa Avenue. Because of the influx of female impersonators, the strip was dubbed "Flounce Row." Because it was show biz, *Variety* reported that the drag queens and kings were appearing in floor shows at joints called "pansy parlors" of the kind that were illegal inside the City of Los Angeles itself, but not illegal outside in that tiny unincorporated area of the County of Los Angeles. It was a county island of queer castaways surrounded by the urban ocean of straight LA. It was where Larry lived and died. It was a beating gay heartland that in 1984 was at long last incorporated as the city of West Hollywood.

As older media folk filling page and screen with the liberating leather discovery that men in their thirties could be hot, they were voyeurs escaping the isolation of their homes in a gay space revered in LGBT history for hosting meetings by early gay activists like themselves from its opening in 1972 to AIDS activists in the 1980s. As gay elders, they liked that politicians such as Governor Jerry Brown often showed up for meetings and rallies with activists who could deliver the gay vote. In fact, Larry often brought his activism home. On April 11, 1973, *The Advocate* published a wonderful photo of Larry working on a political campaign. Groomed camera-ready like a suave 1950s movie star, he was pictured hosting the doomed future San Francisco Mayor George Moscone who was assassinated alongside Harvey Milk in 1978. The photo caption read:

> State Senator George Moscone (D-San Francisco) speaks at a cocktail party in the Los Angeles home of outgoing H.E.L.P., Inc., President Larry Townsend (right) and Fred Yerkes on Friday, March 9. The get-together was arranged through the Alice B. Toklas Memorial Democratic Club of San Francisco and was co-hosted by Jim Foster, president of the club. "The gay community needs a champion," said Sen. Moscone, and he pledged to act as such if he is successful in his campaign for governor of California in 1974.

At the French Quarter, the male half of Noah's Ark streamed around and through the tables of the noisy restaurant where anti-war activist and gay-rights ally Eartha Kitt, the Broadway star famous for her songs "C'est si bon" and "Santa Baby," could be spied eating an Insalata Caprese with students from Lee Strasberg's Method Acting School just across the street. The bustling arcade of first-floor boutiques like "Baby Jane of Hollywood" sold movie posters and memorabilia, and "Dorothy's Surrender," just to the left of the front door, sold rainbow trinkets, and greeting cards, and some of Larry's publications in spinner racks. Larry's friend, publisher Dave Rhodes's business office for his gay tabloid *The Leather Journal* took up three-quarters of the second floor. While dining, many a man kept a knowing eye on the hot muscle parade entering the medical storefront operated at the rear of the first-floor tables by the popular doctor Walter Jekot who in a fascinating Hollywood scandal was indicted on twenty-seven counts charging he was doing a brisk walk-in business prescribing steroids to the muscle crowd we loved for whom nature was not nurture.

Open from eight in the morning to three the next morning, the restaurant was a runway of styling exhibitionists of every race and gender in drag or leather or muscle-shirts who made for an always interesting floor show for the diners who in that Hollywood Babylon liked to survey the passing trade that was often for hire. The actor Thomas Jane, action-hero star of *Boogie Nights* and *The Punisher*, said that in his early days in Hollywood in the 1980s, he, like James Dean in the 1950s, was not adverse to walking up and down Santa Monica Boulevard waiting for someone who would buy him a sandwich.

Larry had bought a sandwich or two as the cost of doing business. He needed pictures to sell his words. He used the French Quarter as a convenient casting couch to recruit handsome vanilla talent willing to pose in leather to illustrate his mail-order brochures and his S&M booklets. The ritual of simply sitting repeatedly at their usual tables empowered their social pleasures: hailing old friends, snubbing enemies, and judging new faces standing by the maître d's plaster-cast fountain. Otto Dix could have painted them sitting at those main-floor tables covered with white cloth under glass. From there they could spy on the foot traffic passing by the murals of Leo Meiersdorff, the New Orleans painter who had bedizened the jazzy walls of the long hall to the toilets where two stalls and three urinals were as busy a dating game as all gay toilets everywhere.

14

JEANNE BARNEY
DAUGHTER OF "THE ELEPHANT GIRL"
THE STRAIGHT WOMAN
AMONG THE LEATHERMEN
QUEER THEORY AND CONSPIRACY THEORY
THE BED OF PROCRUSTES

In the five-person peerage of Larry Townsend and his quartet, Jeanne Barney was the only woman, the only straight person, and the only parent. She had a daughter about whom she never spoke. She also happened to have royal Hollywood roots in grandparents who had been successful silent film actors. I'm reporting the genealogy that Jeanne Mastin-Washburn-Chesley-Barney, she of the multiple surnames who had more aliases than Larry, told me. Her Chicago-born grandfather, matinee idol Bryant Washburn, appeared in 350 films between 1911-1947. His first wife, her grandmother, actress Mabel Forrest, appeared in several leading roles in the 1920s before they divorced in 1928 after fourteen years and two sons. Jeanne's Chicago-born father was Joseph Grabiner Mastin (1921-2005), an artist and draftsman who had a side hustle as a bookie. For fifty-nine consecutive years her mother, the painter Irene Spencer (1916-2006), was serially married to, divorced from, and lived with Joe Mastin who died on Christmas Day 2005, three weeks before Irene herself died on January 17.

Jeanne Mastin was born in the summer of 1938 in Chicago where her mother, who had begun studying at the Art Institute at age nine, survived the Depression by traveling two years with the circus as the Elephant Girl (who rode the elephant), drawing maps for Rand McNally during World War II, and then becoming a newspaper cartoonist before beginning her fine art career in 1964 writing and illustrating children's books while Jeanne was becoming a columnist in the gay press. In 1980, *Plate World: The Magazine of Collectors Plates* described Spencer, beloved for her mother-and-child portraits on china, as "one of the most prolific and popular of women plate artists since Sister Berta Hummel."

Jeanne called her mother, who chronicled Jeanne's early life artistically in her treasured baby book, her best friend. She did years of eldercare for her father and her mother who both died six months before Larry's Fred died in July 2006. Bonded even more while grieving the deaths of her parents and his spouse, Jeanne and Larry struggled together through the Thanksgiving and Christmas holidays and the incoming New Year of 2007.

On the tenth day of that bitter-cold January of 2007 in Los Angeles, Mark Hemry shot an outdoor photograph of Jeanne, Larry, and me that I treasure for its personal intimacy. He posed us grouped together on a stone bench, all three of us joking and laughing, on the steps of the Dorothy Chandler Pavilion, the former home of the Academy Awards, at the LA Music Center where Larry had driven us. While we camped and tangled ourselves into each other's arms, he framed together for the first and only time the founding LA editor of *Drummer*, the founding San Francisco editor of *Drummer*, and the famous novelist who was a *Drummer* columnist.

Despite her public life in gay publishing, Jeanne, divorced from the journalist Frank Chesley, was an intensely private and furtive person, a quadruple Virgo with a stubborn moon in Taurus, a dress-size zero, a fan of Roscoe's House of Chicken and Waffles, an unrepentant smoker with crushes on Frank Sinatra and Daniel Craig, a "Friend of Bill W" at Alcoholics Anonymous since 1984, a passionate animal-rights activist who rescued dogs like her Chinese Crested named Suessie after Dr. Seuss, and a satirist who dubbed her home "Wit's End."

When asked how often she had been married, she always said, "More than twice." When asked how many cats she had, she said, "More than two." When asked about her birthday, she warned, "Never fuck around with a quadruple Virgo." When asked how to deal with an alcoholic friend, she answered from her own experience with Larry in *Grunt* magazine: "If you can't stand this guy when he's drunk, and you can't stand him when he's sober, maybe he'll be easier to tolerate if you're drunk."

As a 1950s high-school teen-queen, she sported Spaulding white bucks with eraser-pink soles and circular skirts with lots of crinoline petticoats. After graduating from the University of Chicago, she sharpened her tongue as a copywriter in Chicago, then San Francisco where she wrote for radio station KSAY, and then LA where she reported for the *Sierra Madre News*. Working as a public relations writer, she figured "advertising could be a force for good in society." So, while watching the rise of gay culture in Los Angeles, she had a pioneering vision of a career opportunity for a straight woman in gay media. The queening of Jeanne Barney was about to begin. In pre-Stonewall 1967, she pitched writing an advice column to Bill Rau and Dick Mitch, the founders of the original *Advocate*. They hired her as one of their founding staff and a continuing contributor until she quit to become the founding LA editor of *Drummer* when Embry hired her in 1975 and got her arrested in 1976.

She was a muse to her friend, the leather artist Chuck Arnett, who, famous for his 1962 leather mural in the Tool Box bar in San Francisco, painted an astounding full-length portrait of the tiny 98-pound Barney encased in her stylish leather boots with legs up to here and gorgeous long hair down to there tucked up under her leather cap. One of her lovers was the pro-baseball player Mickey McDermott, a drinking buddy of Jack Kerouac. She loved Dorothy Parker and Somerset Maugham whose transcendental novel, *The Razor's Edge*, was the book, she wrote me, "that most changed my life."

Having been injured in the 1994 Northridge Earthquake, she profiled herself as an alcoholic in a June 4, 1995, letter to the *LA Times* offering to donate her quad cane to a man the *Times* had featured in a sob story. She wrote:

> In the pass-it-on spirit of Alcoholics Anonymous, of which I have been a clean and sober member for 10 ½ years, I have a quad cane (the kind that stands on its own four feet) which I will happily pass on to Chris Sylbert. I used it for only a short while last year, following

a six-month hospitalization for injuries suffered in the January earthquake—and I would be delighted to see it go to a good home.

She explained to me that she had been standing on a three-foot-tall stool, photographing her damaged chimney for insurance purposes when an aftershock struck. "I went down—splat—on the driveway."

Surviving Larry's death, his "leather wife" becoming his "leather widow," noted about her own health and vigor in 2008:

> I'm still running with scissors and accepting candy from strangers. Just don't call me "Gee-Anne." And when I pass, I want my obituary to shout out, "She succumbed after winning a long struggle with life."

Could Joan Didion have made a picnic of this eccentric salon whose authenticity was more colorful than fiction? I've always appreciated the brief "Introduction" Didion wrote to *Some Women*, a 1989 book of photographs by my former bi-coastal lover, Robert Mapplethorpe. Robert loved shooting leatherfolk in San Francisco, but he had no interest in shooting these LA players. If he had shot Larry and Jeanne for *Some Leatherfolk*, well, what an introduction Didion might have penned about her urban peers.

Jeanne was the most sophisticated, and was a woman famous for editing *Drummer* and for hosting leather functions and fundraisers. In 2006, Mark and I sent her a copy of *Play It as It Lays* because of all of the five, she was the most likely to appreciate a novel—with four narrators, written by an LA woman about a woman in LA—that mirrored their own panic, alienation, micro-aggressions, and sexual psychology. She was respected. The Reverend Troy Perry, founder of the Metropolitan Community Church, said in 2007:

> There were many heterosexuals who helped us in the beginning, but Jeanne Barney was the first to help in Los Angeles. I tell everybody that. I'm so grateful.

She was also, despite some conservative-male reactions, the first and only woman to frequent the leather bathhouse Manspace, 5524 Santa Monica Boulevard, and was the only woman allowed to attend the invitation-only Full Moon Nights at the coincidentally named Larry's Bar, 5414 Melrose Avenue, which she pictured in *Drummer*, issue 4. When the Hawks Motorcycle Club honored her as "Humanitarian of the Year" at its Leather Sabbat in 1976, Rob Clayton photographed her, stylish in a mini-dress, for *Drummer* 11, page 25.

After college in 1961, she said that she, like Larry, got a government security clearance so she could write freelance for the conservative military newspaper, *Stars and Stripes*. When that didn't suit her, she turned to working with resistance groups like the Black-civil-rights and anti-war Peace and Freedom Party. She burned draft cards and bras in the street where crowds of young men ogled the free show. In an effort to syndicate herself during the Vietnam War in 1971, she began writing for the *Grunt Free Press*, the rag-paper alternative magazine full of military jokes, crude cartoons, and bare breasts for Vietnam veterans. Published in Agana, Guam, *Grunt* had an international circulation. Jeanne wanted to title her advice column in *Grunt* with the same title she was currently using in *The Advocate*, "Smoke from Jeannie's Lamp," but *The Advocate* said *no*; so she dubbed it "Genie Speaks" and used her real name as her byline. After exiting *Drummer* in 1976, she once again re-titled her column in 1977 as "Jeannie's Lamp" for the gay paper, *The Montrose Star*, in Houston, Texas.

She wanted *Drummer* to be *The Evergreen Review*. However, that was a content-and-style bridge too far for her LA walkers conceived or born in the 1920s and 1930s who were businessmen focused on "big box-office" profits rather than art and literature for their 1970s magazines, books, and films. She wrote me about John Embry's concept for *Drummer*.

> He wanted a cash-cow stroke book; I wanted a literary stroke book because I thought people into leather were not without an intellectual dimension.

Always playing the part she needed in order to make a living in this boys' club, she, who was identified as "a housewife from La Crescenta" by the *Philadelphia Gay News*, marketed her buddies through the synergy of Embry's *Drummer*. She published Larry's fiction, and featured *Drummer* columnist Fred Halsted's second film *Sextool* on the cover of the second issue, and Earl and Legrand's leather cherry-popper fisting film, *Born to Raise Hell*, on the cover of the third; and Chuck Arnett's drawing of a leatherman on the fifth. She edited *Drummer* from June 1975 to December 1976, before it was rebranded in San Francisco, but she was Larry's "leather wife" who told me that, always defending Larry, she called herself "Larry's Bulldog."

Jeanne was one of three women involved in the *Drummer* origin story. Dagmar King was the first art director, and soon disappeared. My friend and co-worker, the jolly chain-smoking Marge Anderson (d. 1985) was the first typesetter who worked at *Drummer* for six years (1975-1981). Jeanne came aboard with them importing her humorous advice column from *The Advocate*, but she was not listed as editor-in-chief until issue three. She was editor for eighteen months and eleven issues in Los Angeles, and not for its whole LA run of seventeen issues, the last six of which Embry edited as his alter-ego, Robert Payne. After 1976, she left no imprint or fingerprints because Embry erased her by blacklisting her for her disloyalty in quitting because she wanted paid. She had no lingering influence in any way on the San Francisco version. In fact, she herself, embittered, wanted nothing to do with it.

Nevertheless, gay pop culture, skimming history seeking female avatars-behind-men, tends to mistake Jeanne for Jeanne d'Arc as if she personally had gestated a quarter-century of evolving style, content, and agenda of all 214 issues—which she did not—of what became the distinctly San Francisco *Drummer* which evolved—as quickly as the new 1970s scene itself evolved—after she exited mid-decade. When my longtime Chicago friends Andy Charles and Anthony DeBlase bought *Drummer* from Embry in 1986, publisher DeBlase, who wore tall riding boots and flared jodhpurs like Erich von Stroheim in *Sunset Boulevard* (1950), wrote in issue 99 that when *Drummer* moved to San Francisco in 1977, the new editor changed its main theme from leather to masculinity. No offense to queer studies, but to correct the zeal of revisionists imagining the fake news of a virgin birth and female continuity at an aggressively male-identity magazine does not diminish Jeanne's very real contributions in the origin story in which facts, context, and human relationships cannot be discarded.

Drummer itself provides a fixed historic timeline of twenty-four years of 214 monthly issues which list an objective nonesuch of authentic dates, names, and topics. There is a myth that Larry founded *Drummer*. He didn't. There is this myth that Jeanne influenced the 207 issues after she quit. Interesting if she had, but she didn't. I know. I was there in the chair in the office in a new city with a new national demographic. While she was also a pioneer contributor during the founding of *The Advocate*, no one claims her contributions influenced every *Advocate* issue thereafter. Just as *Drummer* contents pages show Larry didn't write for the magazine until 1980, Jeanne contributed nothing in text or subtext after April 1976 , although issues she touched ran through December. There is no internal evidence in the pages of *Drummer* to support claims to the contrary. While Jeanne loved a good fight, female empowerment legends, no matter how sincere, are not gay history.

As a hired participant in the resettlement of the immigrant-refugee *Drummer* in San Francisco, I first learned of this Barney-Embry feud from Embry, with more privy details from Larry, and then years later from Jeanne whom I succeeded as Embry's editor-in-chief in San Francisco from March 1977 to January 1980. During those three years, she, whom I had not yet met or talked to, stayed silent in LA while Embry attacked her inside my *Drummer* issues. He kept her estranged from all of us. In fact, while I continued contributing writing and photography to *Drummer* for twenty more years after my editorship, Jeanne and I, tangled in the net of Embry's casting, didn't meet until January 1, 2006, when, fulfilling my New Year's resolution, I thought one of us should finally break the ice. I picked up my phone in Northern California and dialed the Los Angeles number (that Larry had given me) to ask if I could interview her for a book I was writing on *Drummer*. She talked for four hours.

Larry, who was the leatherman behind the vanilla woman, and was the constant referee between Embry and Barney, appreciated Jeanne's bold strokes in helping Embry design the physical format of the magazine's standard layout of features, fiction, reviews, and editorial columns. But where form needs content and content needs an authentic voice, she was not herself a leather player, thinker, or writer—like Larry whose cult of personality rivaled her cult of personality. She was her genuine self, but lacked that kind of participatory authenticity in a men's adventure magazine famous for the authenticity of its first-person narratives in the style of the New Journalism.

It must be remembered that Jeanne was working as a vanilla columnist for *The Advocate* when Embry first approached her in 1975. He had founded his small pulp-zine version of *Drummer* all by himself in November 1971, and collaborated on his second version as *H.E.L.P.Drummer* with Larry in 1972, three years before he hired Jeanne to come aboard as staff editor for the larger slick-paper version. *Drummer* was her job, not her mission. She was moonlighting. She did not have a leather eye which today would be a leather gaze. But then, in the 1990s, neither, by her own admission, did the non-leather film director Wickie Stamps, the female editor and "butch gent" who bravely, but unsuccessfully, tried to save *Drummer* from going out of business on her watch in 1999. Fifteen years after Barney, Stamps edited twenty-five issues (182-208) to Jeanne's eleven.

To Jeanne's true credit, she and Embry created a working blueprint for a leather magazine, based on Larry's *H.E.L.P.Newsletter*, that by the post-arrest issue eleven spun out of her orbit when she—abetted by advice from Larry who disliked *Drummer* at that time—cut ties with Embry who then warned subscribers away from doing Leather Fraternity mail-order business with her. His continuing revenge when he denounced her in my *Drummer* 30, June 1979, page 38, was one of the reasons I quit as editor six months later. Two issues after her Cycle Sluts feature, she washed her hands of the whole *Drummer* affair. And vice versa. Truth be told, she, who was an irritable smoker, drinker, and divorcee, quit long before *Drummer* left LA because of the irreconcilable differences over the stroke-book nature of *Drummer*, and because Embry owed her thirteen thousand dollars in back pay.

Beginning with *Drummer* 19, the remaining 207 issues of *Drummer* published in San Francisco were, in actuality, re-imagined, and developed post-Jeanne by two publishers after Embry, and by dozens of male, female, and transitioning editors like Pat Califia (issues 173-176), and by thousands of contributors, including Larry, who added seriously focused kink and fetish and male gender identity to the thrust and contents of the rather fluffy original LA version of the leather magazine that Embry had begun as a local bar rag with ads for toupees and the Bla Bla Café in Studio City. On their own terms in the fast evolving pop-culture sex scene of the 1970s, the post-Barney contributors created the archetypal *Drummer* that fans now think of as classic *Drummer*. Jeanne? They built beyond her whose name most of them did not know, and whose work in *Drummer* they had not read.

And yet among leather originalists like Larry, she was, for all the dice she rolled, a part of our *Drummer* Salon forever. In leather history, for all the credit she fully deserves for her midwifery in the delivery of the infant *Drummer*, she, whom I adored, still has the gravitational pull of the moon because people fancy the idea of the Great Woman behind the Great Man whether true or not.

Jeanne wrote me September 2, 2006, about Larry, the man she called "Mr. Willful": "He told me at dinner last evening that if I were a boy, he'd take me to bed." Something they never did.

In that same January 2007, Mark Hemry shot several color photos of the little tribe—threatened with extinction—posed in its very own Natural History diorama at the French Quarter picturing Jeanne, Terry, Roger, and me seated around a blue-gingham-laid table with Larry holding down the center seat—his sad face drooped and depressed after his first Christmas and New Year's as a widower. This photo, minus John Embry, is an historic shot of some of the people who made original *Drummer* happen. Larry had only nineteen months to live.

15

JEANNE BARNEY: LARRY'S "LEATHER WIFE"

Through the years, the stylish petite Jeanne Barney remained the only woman at that French Quarter table of increasingly plump old men whose bumptious nostalgia for their good old salad days had decayed into competition, bragging, and attitude.

On December 29, 2006, six months after Fred's death, Jeanne, whose email address was HollywoodCatLady@, wrote:

> The Day After Christmas. Larry actually did go to lunch with me and John Embry and his partner. I rode with John because Larry didn't decide to go until the last minute; I think that he realized he'd have no one to go to dinner with if he didn't go with us to lunch. It was a not unpleasant couple of hours. John and Larry were in truce mode and promised to stop sticking pins in their respective voodoo dolls. John said that you'd sent him a check for $200 because you wanted to use/reprint something that he didn't remember writing... Not surprisingly, Larry called later in the afternoon to ask what I thought, and whether Embry had said anything bad about him after he left.

That same Christmas, which was four years after the death of Harry Hay, pioneer founder of the Mattachine Society and the Radical Faeries, John Embry gifted Jeanne with the set of pearls the fey Hay frequently wore. She wrote that Embry said about his purchase at auction: "Real estate has been very good to us."

A year later, on December 24, 2007, she wrote me the day after the latest of the traditional Christmas luncheons:

Brunch went well. I realize that now I've accepted the fact that I'll never get my $ out of him, and [that] if I don't have to spend much time with him, he's bearable. I do wish, though, that ...[he] would not regale me with stories of costly remodeling and brand-new LG appliances for...his apartments.

If a plus-one guest, say, Fred Halsted (1941-1989 suicide) or Oscar Streaker Robert Opel (1939-1979 murder) or me (b. 1939), was present to provide a captive audience for these leather pioneers, the performances were even more serrated. Talk about death by a thousand paper cuts. Were they high on smog? What disconcerting fun they were slicing and dicing and bragging and complaining and agreeing on their addiction to mutual abuse. They were wits halfway between Theater of the Absurd and Theater of Cruelty. And then they'd all go out to lunch. Again. And again. An observer could see they were a chosen family of busy folks, jealous and prideful, and lucky, by age and fate, that they had made their own pioneer reputations in the 1960s and early 1970s before there was fierce competition for gay media power in Los Angeles where it took from 1967 to 1974 for Bill Rau and Richard Mitch's local rag, *The Pride Newsletter*, to grow itself—using the appeal of dozens of Larry's opinion pieces and Jeanne's advice columns—into conservative investment banker David Goodstein's national mag, *The Advocate*. In 1974, for the first time outside *The Advocate*, Jeanne and Larry were billed together as star authors on the cover of the first issue of *ERA: The Magazine of the New Age*.

I fancied them all because to me, born a sucker for bohemian eccentricity, they were like matured versions of the kind of colorful Beatnik-bongo-ish types I had come out expecting to meet in coffee houses in August 1957 when I first hit Greenwich Village. But they weren't artists. They were commercial writers, who, like Larry—who wrote his *Handbook* in six weeks, but only after first signing a contract—weren't exactly artists who were writers the way Mapplethorpe was first an artist who became a photographer—to the distress of other competing photographers who were not artists. Their realization of that esthetic "class distinction" may have been one of the many things that fueled their collective emotions in taking their frustrations out on each other in their traveling vivisection show.

They had a special tension. A special anxiety. Even while they were on the inside of gay media, they were always on the outside looking in. They were midcentury hybrid folk straddling history before and after Stonewall. As a writer for the *Journal of Popular Culture*, I saw them as LA provincials forced to change with the incoming international revolutionary 1960s and the new LGBT rising consciousness. In the 1970s, their lucky gay-power boat rose with the rising tide of LA pop culture that Ronald Brownstein documented in *Rock Me On The Water: 1974: The Year Los Angeles Transformed Movies, Music, Television, and Politics*. They were, with their implicit leader Larry, a snapshot of that unique age group who, post-World War II, having come out in the persecuted homosexuality of the 1940s, 1950s, and 1960s, were forced to graduate to the liberated homosexuality of the 1970s if they wanted to be relevant and sell their wares on page and screen.

Maybe it was gay liberation's forcible process of change around their buttoned-down 1950s core values, content, and style that made them nervous and quarrelsome. Perhaps it was their birth years in the Prohibition 1920s and Depression 1930s that made them all so tightfisted with money—the cause of some of their fights—and drove them hard to make a buck out of 1970s gay life, art, and politics. Their generation lived teeter-tottering on both sides of the stone wall of the 1969 gay rebellion which changed gay values and character overnight the way Virginia Woolf wrote in her essay, "Mr. Bennett and Mrs. Brown": "On or around December 1910, human character changed."

They faced for better and worse what Joan Didion played up and laid down in her devastating novel of people coming undone, and being swept away by history, published six months after Stonewall. They were who they were in the pop-culture revolution of the 1970s. The French Quarter was not their Les Deux Magots. They were like a gay Rotary Club of business people making a living by manufacturing gay pop culture they struck off each other for their books, magazines, and films in the way that Fred Halsted spun Didion's 1970 title, *Play It as It Lays*, into the 1972 title for his S&M leather-and-fisting film *LA Plays Itself* which since 1974 has been in the permanent collection of the Museum of Modern Art. As character actors, they were perfect for both Didion's and Halsted's Hollywood. To me, born a half-generation after Townsend and Embry, and a year after Barney, they had a mystique as tragicomic characters, historic heroes even, caught up in the midcentury war between bigots and faggots like bruised characters suffering in a gay novel writing itself against all odds during those degrading and horrible decades of 1950s homophobia, 1960s politics, 1970s police persecution, and 1980s AIDS that drove some people to all kinds of creation and self-destruction.

Tangent to this core circle, Jeanne Barney and I carried on our own snug relationship by landline phone and email for many years in which she often reported the antics of the latest "lunch... between your friends Larry and John." (She always pretended they were my friends.) When the *Leather Journal* announced her as recipient of its Pantheon of Leather Lifetime Award in spring 2008, I was asked to write her Honorary Biography which—aware of her volatility around Larry and John—I sent her for her approval. She liked it until she didn't until she did until she didn't. Over the years, Mark and I had gifted her with purses and perfumes and, from J. Peterman whose unique clothing she fancied, a silky hand-embroidered Japanese jacket we suggested she wear to walk the Leather Carpet at the Leather Archives & Museum ceremony on July 20 in her hometown of Chicago. Instead she decided to stay in LA because her health at best was always fragile. She was, in fact, that summer of Larry's final act, suffering a rolling grief that her dear friend, Stuart Timmons, the fifty-one-year-old co-author of *Gay L.A.* and author of *The Trouble with Harry Hay*, was confined in a convalescent home after suffering a massive stroke on January 31.

On May 31, 2008, while she and Mark and I were lunching for hours over her vegetarian reuben sandwich and our pastrami reubens at Canter's Deli at 419 N. Fairfax where she, in a kind of Hollyweird Canter-bury tale, told us she had sprinkled her father's ashes inside and outside the restaurant two years before, Mark asked her, "What's with you and Larry? Why do you all treat each other like that?" She said he was the second person to ask her that in a week, but she dodged any reason why, leaving the question open to future social historians and literary detectives.

16

LITIGIOUS LARRY: IS A LAWSUIT HARASSMENT? SOCIAL JUSTICE PIONEER, BUT NOT OLD GUARD

Larry began his pioneering activism in the LA politics of gay liberation in the early 1960s working in personal good company with gay rights pioneer Morris Kight, director of the Gay Community Services Center; W. Dorr Legg aka Marvin Cutler, author of the 1956 handbook, *Homosexuals Today*, and founder of ONE, Inc; Jim Kepner, *Drummer* reviewer-columnist and core contributor to the ONE Archives; the Reverend Troy Perry, founder of the Metropolitan Community Church; and super-attorney Albert Gordon, the Drummer Slave Auction defense attorney, who was the litigious Larry's favorite among all the many attorneys he consulted to protect his interests over the years, because he loved lawyers more than he hated them. And he supported them. In 1972, he received a letter of gratitude from attorney Vincent Bugliosi, the prosecutor of Charles Manson and the author of *Helter-Skelter*, for donating big bucks to his campaign for LA District Attorney.

By academic popular-culture standards, *The Leatherman's Handbook*, self-published when Larry was 42 in 1972, is a unique and valuable time-capsule study written by a military and university-credentialed participant. Following his father who was a spy, Larry was a second-generation collector of intelligence spying on gay life and customs with his questionnaire seeking the most private personal data. Ten years later in 1982 to write *The Leatherman's Handbook II*, the LA author repeated internationally for the sequel what he had done nationally for the original. He sent out 6,000 sex questionnaires to his mailing list and received 1,238 responses from individuals (1149 white; 19 Black; plus "others") and from members of groups like the Chicago Hellfire Club and the Gay Men's S-M Activists (GMSMA) of New York.

He was encouraged by the pop success of Dale Brittenhouse's *The Lesbian Handbook* (1966) and Angelo d'Arcangelo's *The Homosexual Handbook* (1968) which he made a point to praise. Even though his queries and conclusions were mostly based on the pre-Stonewall leather culture of leather males, leatherfolk of all genders—ranging from female leatherbois to FTM reviewers—have for years, according to a diversity of fan letters in his files and responses at live conferences, read, enjoyed, learned, and adapted to themselves the basic tropes and codes of the leather lifestyle from his tutorial writing.

The second *Handbook* was immediately famous because of the first. It received positive reviews from influencers and reviewers like Pat Califia, who, later transitioning to Patrick Califia, wrote in *The Advocate*, October 27, 1983:

> Townsend is warm, straightforward, and personal.... which makes it easier for the reader to deal with any difference he or she might have with the author's politics or view of S&M technique....Townsend need not have mentioned women at all, since this is a book for gay leathermen. However, he does...As a leatherwoman, I should be grateful, but it's a little discouraging when my brothers seem to know more about straight women than they know about us female queers.

Especially when the gay press was young and desperate for bespoke material in the 1970s, editors relied on Larry as a sturdy and steady content provider. They exploited his famous boldfaced name, as had Embry, to attract readers by publishing dozens of his political and advice columns, and by headlining generous reviews of his books. His fan base included grateful magazine and newspaper professionals who took the time to send him press clippings of his reviews and columns, and to write letters to pay their respects because he was dependable in delivering good copy to them on time. Even something simple as a note dashed off by Ann Fleming, the features editor at *OUT* magazine, owned by

The Advocate conglomerate, kept him motivated: "Contributing writer Ken Bowling really enjoyed your work." Larry would have had a fit in 2018 when Adam Levin, the owner of Pride Media, the parent company of *The Advocate* and *OUT*, was denounced by the Human Rights Campaign for donating cash to anti-LGBTQ Republican state senators.

Only perverse reactionaries would disrespect him as old guard, or fault the time capsule of his *Handbook* for voicing a vintage 1972 point of view and not a latter-day politically-correct perspective. His years of monthly magazine columns prove he kept on trend with evolving times and issues.

17

COMING OUT IN 1950s LOS ANGELES
THREE MONTHS OLDER THAN JAMES DEAN
CRUISING THAT FAMOUS L.A. GAS STATION
FOR SEX

Larry was my platonic friend for almost forty years, and for all his gruff demeanor, he was so alive and kicking and contrary he was always interesting. He was a contentious West Hollywood superstar whom friends dealt with, and fans adored. Mindful of his public image, and constantly in search of an author head-shot that matched his idea of himself, he drove from Los Angeles to my home near San Francisco in 1995 and asked me to shoot him in a series of pictures, with and without his newest Doberman named "Mueller."

Thirteen years later, during the last desperate spring of his life, he insisted he needed a new author photo so that Mark could re-start his website for him after he had let his ownership of his original domain name lapse. He also feared prosecution from new witch-hunt rulings from the U.S. Attorney General designed to cripple photographers who were suddenly required to have at least two proofs of identification plus a witnessed release to prove their models' ages. Following the former protocols, he had no more on file for his archive of photos than a signed model release. It also depressed him that the internet claim-jumper who had bought LarryTownsend.com would not sell it back to him, he said, for less than a king's ransom. When his new head-shot by an LA photographer arrived in Mark's email, Larry wanted to Photoshop the truth of the original image. In Hollywood where the close-up is everything, and Hurrell lighting is something, he looked in the mirror of the photo and saw a vulnerable old man.

In 1996, when Larry asked me to write an "Introduction" to the forthcoming "Silver Anniversary Edition" of his *Leatherman's Handbook*, I profiled him with the essay, "Leather Dolce Vita, Pop Culture, and the Prime of Mr. Larry Townsend." The next year working together, we won the 1997 National Small Press Book Award for Erotica for the S&M anthology I wrote and he published: *Rainbow County and Other Stories*. Linguistically, he was one of the earliest leather authors coining portmanteau keywords tying *leather* and *sex* and *men* together to form the standard vocabulary of *leathersex* and *leathermen*.

Miffed at the queenstream's relentless civil war of disinformation against leather males, including that which would become a kind of alleged institutional misandry at *The Advocate*, he continued to call out politically-correct leather-haters as he had in his purposeful opening paragraph in his own 1972 "Introduction" to *The Leatherman's Handbook*:

> There have been many books printed over the last few years dealing with various aspects of homosexual behavior and lifestyle. In all of these the leatherman is constantly neglected—neglected or ridiculed by the fluff or the "straight" reporter who wrote the book. In reading these previous efforts...I have been more than a little annoyed. So have many of my fellow leather people.

There is a pop-culture timeline for the always sassy man born during the Depression, a generation before the post-war baby boom which became what publisher Dave Rhodes dubbed the "Leather Boom" of twentysomethings who came out into their gay-male gender identity in the 1970s. In degrees of separation, Larry was only three months older than James Dean who in the 1950s shared the screen with Elizabeth Taylor who shared the screen with Montgomery Clift who shared "that lover" with Larry.

Cruising LA streets and freeways in the 1950s, driving the circuit that locals had called "the Run" since World War I, Larry knew a thing or two about Scotty Bowers' Richfield gas station at 5777 Hollywood Boulevard with its drive-in sex service to the stars, including Monty Clift. Its dynamic fascinated Alfred

Kinsey who once spent a week observing the action for *The Kinsey Report* (1948). Larry acknowledged in *The Leatherman's Handbook* that the toilet for Cinema, the leather bar where he officially came out at twenty-five, was not in the tiny Cinema building, but was next door in the adjoining gas station.

Saying in his lovely requiem for Cinema that he "was just old enough to get in," he mis-remembered, I think, the actual location of that pre-historic leather bar. He recalled it being on Santa Monica Boulevard when it was likely, because of archival evidence and testimony from original Satyrs interviewed about their favorite bar by Kate Kraft at Yale, on the corner of Melrose Avenue and Gower. Having worked with several of his manuscripts over the years, I know he was no more a proofreader of his own texts than he was a fact-checker. Everything he self-published was a first draft written off the top of his head. He wrote: "The john [for Cinema] was outside in the gas station." I'm no Hollywood detective able to solve this mystery, but how many bars near sex-tolerant filling stations could there be in that neighborhood? He dropped a clue in 1972 when he wrote: "The site [of Cinema] is now some kind of tire repair shop." Gas? Tires? It all kind of fits the style around that corner location.

In 1965, when Larry was thirty-five, Scotty's Richfield Station closed to become Christie's Richfield which in 1973 became the Hollywood Arco Station. For fans of Stuart Timmon's WEHO Walking Tours, urban renewal replaced that final third Arco at 5777 Hollywood Boulevard with Fire Station 82 in 2010. Was it close to Cinema? At the ONE Archives at the University of Southern California, I found but one lonely listing for Cinema bar. Logged in as "1960," it was a matchbook printed discreetly with two code words, *Cinema* and *Melrose*, with no street number. At his urging, Dave Rhodes and I theorized from the keyword *Melrose* and from Satyrs history that the long-lost Cinema bar was likely founded around 1953 at what became a perpetual gay-bar legacy address, 5574 Melrose at Gower, and was, like as not, the world's first leather bar.

It was, of course, "very Larry" that he would come out in 1955 at the very model of a modern major leather bar. As a pioneer living inside leather history, he had the luck, the knack, and the talent of a writer in the right place at the right time. The way he studied books on sadomasochism he studied leather life at the foundational Cinema which he described in his 1972 *Handbook* as the platonic ideal of a leather bar. It gave him ideas, credentials, and hands-on experience while he hung out with the first generation of post-war gay bikers whose vintage faces, voices, aura, and fuckery can be seen on YouTube in the documentary *Original Pride: The Satyrs Motorcycle Club* (2005).

As an eyewitness participant in our leather roots, Larry, like *Drummer*, helped create the very leather culture he reported on. In 1969, the changling bar first anchored at that iconic Melrose address became the Arena until 1973 when it became Griff's (owned by a Satyr) where in 1976 Larry attended the first known leather wedding whose two grooms *Drummer* then featured kissing on the cover of issue seven.

Sorting history, of course, is all *Rashomon*; but the historically important one-story brick-and-mortar building that may have been Cinema at 5574 Melrose, located next door to an autobody shop (with its toilet), was a five-minute drive from Scotty's gas station at 5777 Hollywood Boulevard. If I were a Hollywood screenwriter mulling this mystery of 1950s leathermen cruising the gayborhood, I'd conflate all these mashed gay *Brigadoon* addresses. Where else but at Scotty's Richfield would a young Larry living in a new tract house in the San Fernando Valley in the 1950s have met Monty Clift?

Larry was a proper upstart rebel with a cause, romancing the Hollywood-and-Vine charisma of Marlon Brando whose blue-collar and rough-trade sex appeal in *A Streetcar Named Desire* (1951) and *The Wild One* (1953) was queering the Hells Angels outlaw-biker scene swarming the Sunset Strip—confusing the LAPD who couldn't keep straight which manly leather riders were fags. Midcentury LA roared with "gay bike gangs" like the Satyrs (1954) and the Oedipus (1958) motorcycle clubs. These men grew up masturbating to the rough sex in straight men's-adventure magazines like *Argosy*, *Saga*, and *Easyriders* that inspired the gay men's adventure-magazine *Drummer*. The first gay easy riders picked bad-boy rebel names. Satyrs were lusty half-beast gods. Oedipus was a motherfucker. Gunning two-thousand pounds of hot steel throbbing between their legs, the gay leathermen rode their Harley hogs out nights in squadrons to city bars. On weekends, like the gay-orgy bikers partying in Kenneth Anger's iconic *Scorpio Rising* (1963), they roared down the freeways to tribal bike runs at wilderness campgrounds which Larry described in detail in the *Handbook*, Chapter 13. In Chapter 8, "The Bike and Its Owner," he admitted he once bought a motorcycle, but sold it because it was difficult to repair and he didn't think it was safe to drive in LA traffic and put his sex life on the line in a crippling accident.

Instead, he drove his Corvette out at nights, stopping to buy little tin boxes of yellow-mesh amyl nitrite poppers at drugstores like Schwab's on Sunset Boulevard, cruising Pershing Square for Marines who, if interested and interesting enough after a drink at the Biltmore Hotel, he brought back to that small starter house he had bought on the G.I. Bill out in the Valley. He wrote that leathermen should prioritize buying their own homes for the sake of the privacy needed around S&M action. Was there any homage to Brando in the name of the last Doberman he bought just months before he died? He called the pup "Brandon." Jeanne Barney quipped in an email:

> He should have named it "Brandy"...so when he ran down the street chasing the runaway dog, he could yell...!

From the 1950s, Larry kept up with gay popular culture in the La-La-Land he loved, making late-evening pit stops at the famous and cruisy Universal News Stand, now gone with the wind, where we sometimes browsed magazines together at the corner of Hollywood Boulevard and 1655 N. Las Palmas. It was a kind of Hollywood version of the outdoor bookstalls, the *bouquinistes*, lined up along the Seine in front of Notre Dame. With its own outdoor magazine racks stretched as long as five parked cars, it was open 24 hours—a Technicolor scene by day and a film noir by night—under a blue awning with white stripes covering thousands of brightly lit international magazines and periodicals inviting leisurely browsing and cruising and knuckle-bumping on the narrow Las Palmas sidewalk. Fred Halsted included footage of it in *LA Plays Itself.*

In among the industry folk and movie stars who pulled up to the street curb to buy *Variety* and newspapers from their hometowns, Larry early on discovered, next to Bob Mizer's self-published *Physique Pictorial* (founded 1951) two new little gay physique and leather magazines, *Mars* and *Triumph* (founded 1962), both self-published by his contemporary, and future friend, Chicago leather tycoon Chuck Renslow, and his lover, the artist Etienne, of Kris Studio whose homomasculine photography, drawings, and mail-order business, like Mizer's Athletic Model Guild mail-order studio in LA, lit a lightbulb over his head.

These first owners of the first gay small businesses that weren't bars, particularly in grass-roots mail-order, created the first nation-wide gay web. They pioneered a communications network of political and erotic writing, art, and photography that educated urban and rural readers about gay liberation, pop-culture entertainment, and sex styles while inviting the readers to express themselves through letters to the editor, and to hook up through Personal Ads describing who they were and what they wanted so they could meet. Paying twenty-five cents a word, they wrote in S&M shorthand. "GWM bottom seeks masc GBM top for TT, WS, VA, and FF. No fats, femmes, phonies." Translated, that means "Gay white male slave seeks masculine gay Black male master for tit torture, water sports, verbal abuse, and fist-fucking."

As a psychologist seizing the moment, Larry was a leather-identity author staking out and mapping gender legitimacy for leathermen un-closeting their virilized homomasculine selves in a Stonewall culture of fey liberation resisting their existence. The novelist whose social actions spoke even louder than his erotic words got up from his desk and practiced his midcentury community spirit in his volunteer work as an activist Democrat and as the founding president of the Hollywood Hills Democratic Club. He also served on the board of the Whitman-Radclyffe Foundation when gay Californians first set about erecting a united political and philosophical platform.

18

TOWNSEND AND EMBRY RIVALRY
WHEN QUEERS COLLIDE
THE SECRET SAUCE OF LEATHERSEX

In 1972, Larry became president of the Homophile Effort for Legal Protection which he helped found in 1968 to defend gays during and after entrapment arrests by the LAPD. He led the founding of the *H.E.L.P. Newsletter*, the yellow-pulp tabloid forebear of the slick and glossy *Drummer* magazine founded in LA in 1975 by John Embry (1926-2010). Larry chose not to accept Embry's invitation to be a co-founder of *Drummer* because, among other reasons in the soul-destroying cage-fighting that was the LA social scene around the peccant John Embry, Larry did not want to bow to a competing gay alpha male anymore than he wanted to be part of a magazine with a hungry deadline needing to be fed every thirty days. Had he wanted that, he could easily have founded his own magazine titled *Leatherman's Handbook* in 1972.

Even so, Larry was basically always involved with *Drummer* and the *Drummer* Salon of talent because he and Embry hate-liked crossing swords to cross purposes. Was it their male chromosomes that destined them to fight to survive like sperm that carry toxic mutations that poison rival sperm? Nearly the same age and build, they found distorted fun-house mirrors in each other. Neither was a *beau ideal*. So their switch from the Los Angeles cocktail-bar scene of the suit-and-tie 1950s and 1960s to the pre-and-post-Stonewall acid-rock bars where being "fat and forty"—the kids' words in a hippie decade that did not "trust anyone over thirty"—was an unwelcome education. When Townsend published his *Handbook*, he was 42. When Embry founded *Drummer*, he was 49. When Barney began editing *Drummer*, she was 37. When I began editing *Drummer*, I was turning 38.

Both average joe's used leather to date out of their league, as did all we average joe's, because in the leather-bar scene, where leather trumps lookism, there was always a surfeit of eager handsome young masochists seeking anyone from Nostradamus to Nosferatu in a leather vest who would master them. They benefitted from the wonderful anti-lookist and anti-ageist ingredient that is the secret sauce of leather joy that adds years to one's sex life.

To captivate interest and signal their top intent in crowded bars, both men wore their keys on the left and dressed simply in leather vests and jackets as was the laid-back custom in the 1970s before expensive and extravagant tailor-made leather wardrobes became the style with 1980s road warriors laced tight into assless leather chaps, girded with big studded belts, and cinched inside vests topped with age-defusing sunglasses and Muir caps.

Like feuding movie stars, Townsend v. Embry was one of the great gay Hollywood rivalries worthy of its own *Baby Jane* feature film. When Larry declined to contribute to the first issue, Embry so wanted—so needed—to market the popular "Townsend" brand that he made a point to review Larry's novel, *Chains,* so he could print Townsend's superstar name on the contents page to buzz up a connection and to imply an endorsement. However, Embry, in true frenemy fashion, had his reviewer, a certain "Cam Phillips"—who was likely Jeanne Barney—trash the novel and the author:

> the author [was] obviously confused; dull sex scenes; Townsend is not a "good" writer in the sense that Christopher Isherwood and John Rechy are "good" writers [This calculated slam inside *Drummer* that Larry was not "literary" was the same slam made by gay mainstream literary mavens.]; he is weakest when dealing with his characters outside of the bedroom, or when he makes them open their mouths for anything other than sexual purposes; and the cover [which Townsend designed] promises an extremely heavy sexual book, but this is definitely not the case.

In short, because Embry wanted a mystique—and a mail-order company—as powerful as Larry's, he co-opted Townsend's name, topics, and mail-order business plan sired out of Mizer and Renslow. In truth, in a corporate takeover by his Alternate Publishing, Inc., CEO Embry hijacked Larry's *H.E.L.P.Newsletter* and *Leatherman's Handbook* into his own monthly magazine, *Drummer*.

So even before I convinced Larry to begin writing his monthly *Drummer* column "Leather Notebook" in 1980, his influence as a leather guru shaped the psyche and content of Embry's iteration of *Drummer* that thrived on Larry's synergy of marketing, initiation, and identity for 1970s men self-fashioning themselves as a new archetribe of homomasculine men in that first decade of gay lib when women were self-fashioning themselves in feminism.

Larry's *Handbook* reported an existing and projected leather lifestyle and thus created even more emerging kink culture—such as kick-starting Embry into creating *Drummer*. Pushing beyond the revelations in the 1948 *Kinsey Report*, his *Handbook* was indeed the first analysis of leatherfolk in the twentieth century. It pairs perfectly, as noted, with William Carney's intense leather-identity novel *The Real Thing* (1968), an epistolary book which Larry admired and cited specifically in his *Handbook*, and imitated in the format of his "Leather Notebook" and "Ask Larry" columns responding to letters from his network of readers. In his archives, Larry saved all his fan mail. In 2012, his niece Tracy Tingle remarked to sex-positive feminist Carole Queen at the San Francisco Center for Sex and Culture:

> There are letters from guys in the early 1970s—resplendent with the vernacular of the day—letters from closeted guys in the Midwest, letters from people in enema clubs...*the letter writers reflected the AIDS epidemic unfolding in what they wrote about and requested* [Italics added]. It was really touching and beautiful to go through some of those.

In a bonding 1972 coincidence caused by leather BDSM ritual and gay-wicca ritual rising together after Stonewall, Larry published his *Handbook* at the same moment my two books touching S&M rites and rituals, *Leather Blues* and *Popular Witchcraft*, were also published. In 1969, before Larry and I met face to face, I received his Kinsey-like sex questionnaire whose fetish answers he used to build his first *Handbook*. I sent him my dozen pages of answers, and added some suggestions about magical S&M rituals. While I then quoted some samples of his questions in *Popular Witchcraft*, he added "Witchcraft and Demonology in S&M" into his *Handbook*. His concluding Chapter 18, "Where Do You Stand?" reprinted the entire questionnaire. His *Handbook* went on to prepare the way for Radical Leather Faerie Mark Thompson's landmark anthology, *Leatherfolk: Radical Sex, People, Politics, and Practice* (1992)—in which Thompson, the former editor of *The Advocate*, included essays by twenty-seven leather authors, including me, while excluding Townsend, Barney, Embry, and Earl.

In 1976, when *Drummer* shook the trust of its masculine-identified readers with that camp cover of the Cycle Sluts shot by streaker Robert Opel, psychologist Townsend told editor Barney he was not surprised to learn of pissed-off men who demanded camp to be taboo in *Drummer* where masculinity was totem. As a unit of desire-as-identity in the mindset of leathermen in the 1970s, the words most repeated in the *Drummer* classifieds in which readers wrote Personal Ads identifying themselves, as well as what quality they were seeking in sex partners, were *masculinity* and *masculine*. It was to that homomasculine choir that Larry preached.

In 2020, Sister Leucrezia of the Toronto Sisters of Perpetual Indulgence, invoked a "Litany of Leather Saints" as a blessing:

> Oh, St. Tom of Finland...Oh, St. Peter of Berlin...Oh, St. Brando of *The Wild One*...Oh, honored Pat Califia...
> In the name of Larry Townsend, may your saddle soap froth eternally, and in the name of Bettie Page, may your pin-up be honored, and your riding crop strike true.

19

SEX PERVERSION, FELLATIO, AND ENTRAPMENT
LAPD COPS BUST LEATHERFOLK

As writer, photographer, and leather personality, Larry Townsend exercised real agency as a *macher* in the evolving gay liberation scene in Los Angeles bars and bike clubs. When he and others founded H.E.L.P., its stellar purpose was to bail out gays entrapped in tea rooms and arrested in bar raids by the LAPD. Larry was particularly motivated. In his FBI file, I found he had been arrested three times: for "Sex Perversion and Fellatio" (1963); for "Failure to Register as Sex Offender" (1964), followed by a 1968 ruling that his registration was no longer required; and for "Lewd Conduct" at the 1972 H.E.L.P. fund-raiser that was dismissed for insufficient evidence the same year he published his *Handbook*.

Held at LA's then-leading leather bar called the Black Pipe, the H.E.L.P. charity event suggested a two-dollar donation at the door. One of the booths on the outdoor patio auctioned off leathermen for a date to raise money to open a gay Community Center. The LAPD decided this was prostitution. This mini-event was a slave auction that preceded the more famous Drummer Slave Auction raided with a vengeance by the LAPD four years later in 1976. That bust was so traumatic, the ten-month-old *Drummer* fled from disaster in Los Angeles to destiny in San Francisco.

Proving no good deed goes unpunished, the cops targeted their so-called "Black Pipe 21" arrests on the President of H.E.L.P. who was Larry Townsend, and on H.E.L.P.'s board of advisors, including, the astonished political worker at the card table registering voters. (Larry was booked under both his names.) In 1972,

Townsend's and Embry's names appeared together for the first time on the masthead of the first issue of the newsprint magazine combining Townsend's *H.E.L.P.Newsletter* with advertising salesman Embry's small zine-version of *Drummer* which Embry had first published all by his lonesome in November 1971. The new title was *H.E.L.P.Drummer*. The urge to merge flopped because in 1973, Larry was deposed as president by Embry causing Larry to resign as an ex-officio member of the H.E.L.P. board of directors in a drop-dead sarcastic letter he sent to Embry, the new president of H.E.L.P.

So Larry began making competitive moves against Embry to land on his own feet politically. In its October 10, 1973 issue, *The Advocate* headlined that David B. Goodstein, president of the San Francisco Whitman-Radclyffe Foundation, had chosen Townsend as its Southern California representative. At the very moment when Embry was founding Alternate Publishing and *Drummer* in 1974-1975, Goodstein was buying *The Advocate*, and Townsend was becoming founding president of that Hollywood Hills Democratic Club which was the first openly gay political club in LA.

In fact, the then really quite groovy Black Pipe bar itself, owned by Dwayne Moller, the chairman of the Tavern Guild political resistance, was a virtual All-American leather-fraternity house bothering no one out on La Cienega near Venice in West LA, a deserted light industrial area similar to San Francisco's South of Market. *The Advocate* headlined "Massive Bar Raid," September 12, 1972. Morris Kight and the leatherish Reverend Troy Perry, helped raise bail for Larry and the others; and H.E.L.P. carried the costs. The charges against Townsend were dropped and the last defendant cleared on June 21, 1974, one year before that hybrid *H.E.L.P.Drummer* with its Personal Ads morphed into Embry's stand-alone *Drummer* magazine.

When *Drummer* was ten-months old, the LAPD repeated the scenario of harassment at the Black Pipe in Chief Davis's infamously political raid on the *Drummer* charity Slave Auction at the Mark IV Bath, 4424 Melrose, on April 10, 1976, when forty-two leatherfolk, including Jeanne Barney, were arrested and charged variously with solicitation for prostitution and with breaking a nineteenth-century law forbidding "slavery" under the penal code title, the "Infringement of Personal Liberty." When the stormtroopers handcuffed Jeanne, they asked her if she was a drag queen. She said, "If I were a drag queen, I'd have bigger tits."

Not to blame the victims, but, insider truth be told to history, the Slave Auction was a premeditated excuse by Chief Davis to bust the fag magazine that couldn't itself be busted because of freedom of the press. Christian conservative Davis loathed the monthly contents Jeanne and John purposely chose to publish in those first issues glorifying gay outlaw bikers, inter-racial sex, fisting, bestiality, piss, necrophilia, coprophagia, prison rape, inept cops, and unsolved sex murders. They taunted him in print as "Crazy Ed." They tried to be provocative, and they succeeded, and suffered from the stress of courtroom drama for three years, the entire time I was editor. While they tried to be debonair in print about the severely homophobic abuse, the emotional trauma of that night stayed with them till they died. Larry, who rallied to their emotional support, was lucky he had not attended the Slave Auction because at that moment he and Embry were not speaking.

In a nicely autobiographical interview for the Leather Archives & Museum in the 1990s, Larry told Joe Laiacona writing as the leather author, "Jack Rinella":

> Fortunately for me, we [Embry and he] had a falling out before the Slave Auction. Otherwise, I would have been there and would probably been arrested [along with Embry, Jeanne, Terry Legrand, and Roger Earl, and forty others]. We [Embry and he] had a terrible squabble.

So, boycotting Embry, Larry spent the evening of April 10 practicing slavery in his own photo-studio dungeon at his home on Sunset Plaza Drive above West Hollywood where many a bound-and-gagged and grateful slave experienced an S&M session feeling Larry's greatest hits while his component-stereo speakers boomed out Mahler's *Sixth* as well as his *Ninth*. (The leathersex was mostly mutual masturbation with, if his arrest record reveals anything, fellatio.) He described his "playroom," and his marital relationship analogously, in a scene in the *Handbook*, Chapter 2, "The M or the S?" It began:

> I pulled into my garage and led Ronnie down the darkened pathway to my "playroom" [which he went on to describe in detail in Chapter 9, "Booze and Drugs"]. As my friend of eight years [Fred Yerkes] is not interested in leather, I have made the lower den into a convertible arena [which later became their television room].

Writing ostensibly about the mixed-marriage of another half-leather couple with whom he said he had just dined, Larry, who was often writing autobiography projected fictitiously on others, wrote in loving code about his own perfectly happy mixed-marriage profiling the vanilla Fred, and what Larry thought Fred thought about Larry's fame:

> I remember, after I left that night, I continued to think about Len's account [of leatherman Len's vanilla husband] and I began to appreciate Augie [Fred] as I never had before. He was a sexually active guy, with no particular interest in leather or S&M. Yet he accepted Len's involvement, probably taking a vicarious pleasure in his friend's [Larry's] exploits...perhaps some pride in his reputation among the other leather people. [Larry loved his reputation.] It simply wasn't his thing, and by choice he went another route. It was for this particular pair of guys, a completely satisfactory arrangement. Each had found the proper counterpart for his own emotional needs. Perhaps it was pure dumb luck, or maybe it was a matter of being mature enough to know when they'd found a good thing. Whatever the reasons, Len and Augie [Larry and Fred] had found the answer. So have many others.

20

LIFELONG COMMUNITY VOLUNTEER
"STUPID AWARDS"
THE LAST SUPPER OF THE
LEATHER PATRIARCH

For almost forty years, whenever a women's or men's leather organization or community fund-raiser invited him to speak on a panel or to read from his work or to judge a leather beauty contest, Larry made it a genuine point of honor to show up to help his hosts succeed. His aura drew fans who genuinely loved him. Larry knew people never forget how you make them feel.

He was honored with several awards from the leather community. In 1995, he received a Lifetime Achievement Award from LeatherFest Los Angeles. That same year he was doubly dignified by the National Leather Association with both its Steve Maidhof Award for literary activism and its Lifetime Achievement Award. In 2000, he welcomed the Special Community Award from Christopher Street West. In 2002 he was iconized with a Lifetime Achievement Award from the Erotic Authors Association, and with a Pantheon of Leather Forebear Award from Dave Rhodes' *Leather Journal*. In 2016, CLAW, the Cleveland Leather Annual Weekend organization, inducted him posthumously into its Leather Hall of Fame. On December 21, 1997, when we were faxing each other weekly, he surprised me when he wrote, somewhat facetiously, complaining about "crap" he had to take from "assholes" for "stupid awards" he "didn't want anyway." He was not ungrateful for his awards and he didn't mean any award in particular when he joked:

Why the fuck doesn't someone give me an award that has a nice substantial check attached to it. How much do you get for a Pulitzer?

Readers appreciated that his *Handbook* was authentically "descriptive" of emerging leather behavior, and not a nasty "prescriptive" book of old-guard "Thou Shalt Not" rules. Matt Johnson, born six years after *The Leatherman's Handbook* was published, acknowledged Larry's permissive latitude in the Leather Archives & Museum magazine, *The Leather Times*, issue 1, 2009:

> Townsend, a prolific writer and shrewd businessman, was able [because he ran his own press, and recycled his titles with other publishers]...to keep much of his work in circulation during his lifetime....three decades in print is an impressive tenure for any book, let alone a non-fiction pulp paperback about a fairly arcane mode of gay sex.... When I first read his *Handbook* [in 1998], I wanted so badly to be told what to do that I completely missed what Townsend was up to: telling us [not what to do so much as telling us] who we are.

Larry's last public appearance and speech was in March 2008 at the Mr. San Diego Leather Appreciation Supper for thirty people hosted by Graylin Thornton, the African-American Mr. Drummer 1993, among whose goals was to make leather more racially inclusive. Larry, Graylin recalled, became "irritated" that evening with a well-meaning guest speaker who, taking the microphone for ten minutes to introduce the Legend, stole his thunder leaving Larry little to add about his life and career. In his address, the author, who would die in four months, expressed his lifelong concern about his wits:

> I'm afraid of losing control. I don't use drugs and I don't drink more than two drinks a night.

In June, just weeks before he died, I published his last piece of writing in *Gay San Francisco: Eyewitness Drummer* in which he documented his personal version of the constant battles fought by the besieged leather community against the LAPD.

He was as much a media celebrity in London and Berlin and Chicago as he was in Los Angeles. In New York at the Mineshaft on February 28, 1982, manager Wally Wallace—whom Larry squired around bars on his visits to LA—feted him like a leather god with a party invitation drawn by Rex who threw down a gauntlet to the guests with a message advising: "The very best way to tell our guest Larry Townsend...that New York knows what he wrote about is to just get down and do it!"

That challenge to action was unintentionally ironic. Larry was there to sell books. He, who talked and wrote a good game, would never have played at the perversatile Mineshaft because he was not a heavy player and was not into drugs. I doubt he ever had naked sex. I can't image Larry Townsend naked. He knew the private Townsend could never measure up to the public Townsend. He understood the other famous Larry, Laurence Olivier, who is said to have quipped what any man could have said that every athletic champion proves a big disappointment once you pull down his jockstrap.

In San Francisco, late in his life, even after the VCR and the internet began making books an endangered species, he could pack a crowd into bookstores. When he and I read together from our new books in the Outspoken Series at A Different Light Bookstore at 18th and Castro on November 9, 1997, the audience, shown on the videotape Mark Hemry shot, loved seeing their hero make an entrance into that legendary bookstore with his Doberman dog on one leash, and a nearly naked young leather-dog slave on the other. When both dog and slave "sat" at his stern command, he brought down the house with cheers and applause.

21

"HE WHO DIES WITH THE MOST COLUMN INCHES WINS!" NIECE SALUTES UNCLE IN *LA TIMES*

Larry was avuncular with fans the way he was Dear Old Uncle—DOU—to his nieces and nephew. On July 31, 2008, his niece Tracy Tingle sent me a copy of the endearing press release she sent to the *LA Times* and the *Bay Area Reporter*. We were comparing notes to coordinate versions of his obituary to reach his variously diverse friends and fans. It was wonderful she submitted her straight personal profile "to give a glimpse of Larry's life" to add unconditional family love to the gay obituary I was writing to profile Larry as a colorful person beloved by real people before his became a soulless or inimical entry in Wikipedia where nothing prevents revisionists from posting specious narratives. I knew that Larry would like all the column inches we could get him. I once told him my little joke: "He who dies with the most column inches wins." His niece felt very honored to be one of the two women (in addition to Jeanne Barney) who had ever seen inside Larry's very private dungeon which he described as a minimalist space in his *Handbook*.

She wrote:

> I was pretty close to my Uncle Larry. He has always "been there" for our family. Despite what would by most seem a very non-traditional lifestyle, he was in many ways quite traditional. He really loved celebrating holidays, Christmas in particular was a favorite. He loved decorating his tree, and putting out all his Christmas "knickknacks." He and Fred were with our family for most holidays while we were growing up in the 60s/early 70s, which I guess was

probably somewhat unusual. They continued to celebrate with us some, but this was made more difficult over the years since we all left living in L.A. We are all resettled in the Bay Area now (Berkeley and Healdsburg), so over the last 10 to 20 years we've had more "family time" with him up here [where Mark and I live].

He (and Fred) enjoyed visits to the Bay Area quite a bit, though Larry would often remark how sad it was that so many men he knew from up here (and everywhere else, of course) had died—many from AIDS. He was always a really dedicated uncle—never forgot birthdays, etc., etc. In the last 15 years or so he started referring to himself as our "Dear Old Uncle." He was also very sweet and thoughtful with my 2 kids and my brother's 2 kids. He always sent them great birthday presents, and loved getting them lots of chocolate things at Easter, and so on. Who knew the big bad leatherman was such a sweetheart, eh? Not to say that he couldn't be extremely opinionated and difficult. He could. We did love to rail against the Bush administration together. He voted for Obama in the primary, by the way. [The general election itself was a hundred days after he passed.]

He was a huge classical music and opera fan/buff. We played classical music for him the last couple of weeks in the hospital—which if he registered it, I'm sure soothed him. [In an earlier email, she had told me: "I kept whispering to him on his hospital bed that if he came through, I'd have a margarita with him...I know how much he loved his little indulgences."]

He was fairly social. He loved to eat and enjoy meals with friends. He and Fred joined a gay men's supper/social club in LA probably about 8 years ago or so, which provided him/them with a lot of enjoyment. His friends and family were really important to him.

He and Fred really loved collecting things—clocks, anything Doberman Pinscher, pigs. His house is full of many of these items. He had a succession of Dobermans (real ones)—really, I think for most of my life (I'm 47) until his last died about 5 years ago. [She hadn't yet heard about his newest Doberman, Brandon.] I can also claim to be one of 2 women who ever saw his dungeon, that used to be in this kind of basement/storage area of his house. (The other woman was a dominatrix who lived up the street). I happened to be at his house for a party with [porn director] Bob Jones, [porn star] Rick Bolton, and a bunch of other guys [young porn actors] from Bob Jones Productions, plus a lot of older gentlemen who were greatly enjoying the company....anyways, there was a group going down to see the famous Larry Townsend dungeon, and my uncle asked if I wanted to go too. Well, duh! It was small, and dark—not as gothic as I had imagined or wanted it to be, I suppose. He did have a collection of some antique restraints there. I suppose such an event was a little lost on me, but I do really like having the honor of being one of two women... One more thing that might be of interest. We are going to put his "archives" (books, artwork, memorabilia, etc.) in the Brown University Special Collections.

As happened, in spite of the astrologer's warning against changing his birth name, Irvin-"Bud"-Townsend-Bernhard-Junior-Michael-Lawrence-"Larry" Townsend, became a star and left a cultural legacy.

22

THE KING LEAR OF LEATHER
"DO YOU STILL HAVE SEX?"
LEATHER WEDDINGS

Writing in the *Bay Area Reporter* for over thirty years, leather columnist Mister Marcus (1938-2009), whose email was the trenchant HatchetQ@, noted that the death of his Los Angeles peer was a loss to the "leather universe." Larry Townsend, big and tall, was a dominant personality who lived life large as a mercurial twentieth-century writer and photographer whose gusty moods could have been charted by the National Weather Service, and whose Rolodex of friends and frenemies might well be turned into a plot with arias like the operas he and Fred attended for years. Six weeks after Larry died, Terry Legrand wrote asking how he might purchase Larry's season tickets. "I'm asking because he was an avid opera fan as I am. He would give me any tickets he did not use during the season." I connected him to Larry's niece. He was too late.

At the Los Angeles Opera, the season after Larry died, a new young couple in stylish clothes, not knowing whom they replaced, smiled as they sat down taking their turn in a treasured pair of permanent seats surrendered only in death by Larry and Fred, the gay couple who through the years rarely missed a production. The incoming millennials would not have known what hardly anyone knew about the man behind the Great Man: the cordial cynic Fred Yerkes, a former accountant at Disneyland Corporation and then a tax expert at Capital Records, who retired in 1995 to manage their domestic life, and their thriving mail-order business office located in the West Hollywood apartment (Suite 502) they owned at 1850 N. Whitley Avenue.

That was also the address where on September 30, 1996, shortly after Fred's retirement, Larry registered their nonprofit "G. Elisabeth Mueller Corporation" named, with typical Townsend drollery, after his current Doberman, Mueller, who was the black dog I photographed with him in 1995. His use of "Elizabeth" was a camp nod to Mel Brooks' 1967 movie, *The Producers*, that satirized Hitler as "Adolf Elizabeth Hitler...who was descended from a long line of English Queens." The film was fresh in Larry's mind because that year it was big news in small talk when it was selected for preservation in the National Film Registry of American films that are culturally significant.

Larry and Fred were two men in love, with a wish to marry, ideally in a ceremony like the one celebrated in Robert Opel's historically important article, "*Drummer* Goes to a Leather Wedding," featuring two LA leather grooms kissing on the cover of issue 7, July 1976. One time in 2002, after a late supper at his nephew's wine-country restaurant in Healdsburg where three of us dined on Ralph's signature Chicken Paillard, we four were kidding around outside on the town square under a dripping awning in the cold on a rainy night, no one wanting to part, and Larry and Fred, together then for thirty-nine years, were being very warm to Mark and me, together for twenty-three years, and from out of nowhere I asked the other couple in badinage, as one does, "Do you guys still have sex?" Shock! Deer in the headlights! Laughter! A flash. A photo. Fred. Eyes rolled up. Camping.

The answer lay, of course, in the *Handbook*, Chapter 10, "Of Friendship and Lovers" in which Larry, described that long-term couple, "Len and Augie," fictional stand-ins for him and Fred:

> These two men have lived together long enough that their love no longer depends upon whatever sexual interactions they have. Neither is there any problem of hurt feelings when Len "does his thing." I was at their home for dinner a few months ago, when Len described his most recent exploit. He did this in Augie's presence, and far from displaying any ill will, his spouse contributed a few details when Len omitted them. I think the experience

illustrates the ease with which the two of them maintain their nearly ideal marriage combination.

Despite his conservative bull-elephant bellowing and belligerence, I remember Larry fondly. He was my dear friend minus sex. At the beginning of our relationship, before I knew many details of his biography, he screamed at me only once when he telephoned and his Caller ID came up on my landline, and in my surprise I asked him, "Who's Irvin Bernhard?" He shouted, "You've been snooping!" So said the Air Force spy. (With Larry, your mileage could vary.) I hadn't been snooping, not even as a journalist: "It came up from your phone." "Fred was supposed to have changed that ID on this line years ago!" I knew he had a birth name, but I was fine knowing him by his chosen name. He apologized next day by fax, and the incident warmed our relationship. In LA, he finally got my San Francisco message that we were to be friends, never frenemies. What was interesting is that he believed his birth name was some kind of a fraternal secret even though, as a point of local controversy, it had been published many times in the LA press, but that was long before there was an internet where nothing is hidden. And what difference did it make?

So, what about the heart of this man born conservative who served as a government spy and then studied *us*? On January 29, 1975, he wrote in his "We, A People" column in *The Advocate* that he was miffed when readers dismissed him as a "Communist SOB."

He admitted that

> they had, however, made an interesting point. As a lifelong Republican, who had yet to change party affiliation, I was regarded by the "radicals" as being just slightly to the right of Attila the Hun...and by gay activists who thought all gayfolk should be "left-wingers"....Now let me make it clear that I do not consider our early activists to be disreputable. I disagree very strongly with the politics of some, if not most, but I respect their courage. All of us are benefitting...from the developments that are following their initial breakthroughs...that could not

have come to pass if someone had not broken the ice and started the whole thing going...

People tend to use the labels "conservative" or "liberal," "Democrat" or "Republican." Yet these no longer define any absolutes (if, in fact, they ever did).

He ended with a grand finale. "While we seem to have found more friends in one party more than the other," he declared in precise words, "there are good guys in both."

If there is a lesson in the cautionary tale of the life of Larry Townsend, it bears repeating that gay men must be careful like straight men not to become angry old men.

In 2008, his professional life was ending as stridently as it had begun with a distrust of politically-correct politics and publishers who wanted to "steal his writing." He thought of himself as a keen part of the LA entertainment industry with its focus on intellectual property and copyright disputes. Thirty-three years before, establishing his lifelong affinity for lawyers whom he clung to, he had bought ad space in *The Advocate* of July 19, 1975, to vent his ire, and piss on his territory. Headlined "Don't Be Ripped-Off," his 1975 anger foreshadowed his 2008 lawsuit against piracy of his work.

> At the present time, four imitations of my privately printed *Treasures of S&M* are being widely distributed mostly through the eastern...United States. I would like my gay leather brothers to know that these are not authorized editions, despite the fact that my name appears on some of them. They are lacking large portions of my original material, and...the [Mafia] hoods who ripped them off used heavier paper to make the books look thicker, but they are little more than half the length of the originals.
>
> [He then jumped on the marketing opportunity.] Although I do not normally advertise my private-edition materials, I feel I must do so now to offer my readers an alternative. [He then listed several bookstores and distributors and wrote in ALL CAPS:] THESE ARE THE ONLY LEGAL, AUTHORIZED OUTLETS FOR

MY MATERIAL. [For his big finish, he added in ALL CAPS under his written signature] AND A "P.S." TO THE HOODLUMS: All of my materials have now been reprinted with copyrights. If you steal anything from me again, I will file a complaint with the FBI.

In 2006, Larry, Jeanne, John Embry, and I mobilized to fight off one ravening wolf of a Midwestern publisher-distributor who, disregarding copyrights, thought that *Drummer*, out of print since 1999, had become gay community property he could reprint and sell the way Larry's books had often been pirated. At that time, Jeanne Barney wrote me about Larry's disarray:

> I know that even Larry can't remember what he published and when—when so many were published so frequently under so many different titles.

Because of this, I began urging Larry to do his housekeeping and to write a bibliography of his feature articles, columns, interviews, books, and photography. It seemed he hadn't updated his records since his first listings of his novels in Chapter 15 of his 1972 *Handbook*. Mourning Fred's death, he was not in the mood to tally his own life's work while his personal life as a dependent, disoriented, and despondent widower fell apart.

In 1972, Larry also began writing the first of his hundreds of mail-order brochures whose catalogue lists can provide a bibliography with vintage thumbnails written by the author.

> GL 142. *The Gooser*. $2.95. First gay novel by Larry Townsend. A mad tale with a touch of humor set during the American Revolution. (Original title: *The Gay Adventure of Captain Goose*)

> GL 150 and GL 149. *Leather Ad :"M"* and *Leather Ad "S."* $2.95 each. A leathersex double-header. Two young men place ads in an underground paper, one as "M," one as "S." Reviewed and recommended by *GAY* (NY) and called the "primers of S&M" by *The Advocate*

PR 259. *Billy's Club*. $1.50. A brutal saga of hustlers, murder, and rough sex; set in contemporary Hollywood. (The author's best?)

So on June 27, 2007, in order to activate Larry's responsible self-defense, I wrote to my acquaintance Sam Streit at the John Hay Library at Brown University:

> Last January in Los Angeles, Mark and I over a five-day period at various restaurants extolled to Larry Townsend the virtues of you and Brown—especially since his partner of forty-four years, Fred Yerkes, died suddenly last July 7, 2006. Apparently our conversation and continuing advice has percolated in the intervening months, and LT called tonight asking for your phone number.... We told him the general info of our good experiences with you and Brown about which he asked specifically to reassure himself... LT, as advised, is interested in leaving Brown the copyright to his works, etc....So I thought to give you his email so you could make contact. I also gave him your email; but he prefers telephone. To be proper, I have cleared this with him so there are no surprises. He is heartily looking forward to getting your email and/or a call.

Sam responded that same day:

> As to Larry Townsend, I'll be happy to talk with him. Curiously, and I wonder if he has forgotten this, we had an ongoing relationship with him for a number of years. He sent us copies of most of his publications (though not films) and sent us new ones as they came out. But, the most recent imprint date seems to be 2003. As you know he is pretty prolific and we have almost 120 entries for him in the library's online catalog. In fact, we quite spiced up the national bibliographic databases by contributing cataloging data for his various works. In any event, I'll be in touch.

I responded minutes later:

So nice to read your words. LT wants to take his relationship to you beyond where it has been in order to fund larger matters such as Brown owning the copyrights to keep his work in print on page or online forever. My Mark Hemry, after much convincing of The Townsend, will be building a simple website for LT later this summer; Mark has had LT prepping his own materials for the last five months. In January, for instance, Mark photographed all of LT's many literary awards to help toward the end of illustrating the site.

A week later on July 4, 2007, I urged Larry:

By the way, have you thought anymore about "The Papers of Larry Townsend" which could be twenty linear feet comprising unsorted boxes and files of original mss, letters, photographs, drawings, etc. collected and archived at John Hay Library Brown U? And your endowment with funds for your papers so they can be collected, shipped, and catalogued by a hired graduate student. Just following up because your life's work is so valuable and such a window into both leather and the LA gay scene since the 1950s. A treasure trove to be mined during the next hundred years plus. Sam Streit is the man at John Hay, Brown, to talk to. Call if you like. We always love to hear your voice.

Archive placement was important to him, but he was conflicted. He had heard the rumors of politically-correct separatist staff and volunteers purging LGBT archives of both gay male and S&M material. Because of his lifetime of harassment and discrimination, he had reasons to believe the gossip. He figured queer life was continuing to conspire against him even as his sun was setting. In his depression, he could not motivate himself to commit his life's work to any institution. Nor, for that matter, could Jeanne. In 2020, her archives were scattered to the winds of eBay.

23

GAY SCANDAL
RAGE AGAINST THE MACHINE
AUTHOR DECLARES WAR ON BOOKSTORES
TEA AND SYMPATHY

Six months later in 2008, the leather lion in winter, raging against the dying light, suffered from a growing anxiety that made him even more aggressive and angry, and put him in a panic at odds with publishers, bookstores, and chums like Embry, and Jeanne who was furious with him for suddenly saying false personal things about her in the way that Embry had in the past said false professional things about her. (It's not easy to sort their true histories.) It was the last act of a bad scene. In Joan Didion's essay, "Slouching Toward Bethlehem," she wrote, "Marriage is the classic betrayal," and it fit Mr. Leather and his Leather Wife. He knew she had aches and pains, but for some reason he dramatically exaggerated her health, telling several people, including Mark and me, that she who was seventy was eighty years old, poor, sick, bipolar, and eating cat food. He hurt her pride. She was furious with him, and miffed that Mark and I, alerted by Larry's distress call which we believed was genuine, sent her an email on April 27 inquiring as delicately as possible if she and her cats were okay.

Trying to patch it up with Jeanne, Larry with a hundred days to live had written to her on April 25:

> I wish things were back to normal with us. I am definitely going ahead with the lawsuit against Herbert [Moseley, publisher, Nazca Plains Corporation] and could have used your advice along the way. The new book [*TimeMasters*, designed by Mark Hemry] is ready. They [Mark] sent the proof yesterday....I haven't been to Fr. Mkt [French

Market] since our last visit because no one is available during the day, and at night everyone wants something else (better?).

He closed saying his sister had found a new Doberman pup for him.

Jeanne responded to him twelve hours later:

> I told you I would be available to help you whenever you needed it. That certainly goes for the Herbert stuff. As for the French Market, that would be loverly. [And then, in one of her characteristic organ recitals in which her illnesses and grief competed with his illnesses and grief, she continued.] Unfortunately, I have been in such rotten shape (and no—I am not now, nor have I ever been, bipolar) that it's all I can do to feed the animals. I've had to send the *Jugend* [her German term for her young male assistant] to the Post Office because I've simply not been able to go out. [She ended with a clap back insinuating he, not she, was the distressed one who was too old and sick to take on a pup.] That's a beautiful dog. Poor boy! He really deserves a good home and lots of love.

An hour later in the soap opera that was fast becoming a reality show, she wrote to me about his lack of attention:

> It's a bit disappointing, but not surprising, that there's been no response to this [her real illnesses]—not even "Do you and the cats have food" or "Is there anything you need at the store?" I guess that, to Your Friend Larry Townsend, "Back to normal" means "Don't bother me with your shit."

On April 30, she wrote to me:

> Larry and I are more or less speaking again. He's driving up north [to Healdsburg] on Monday to pick up the Doberman. I told him again what a bad idea I thought it was, for him, and for the dog. "But I *waaaant* it," he said. Then he told me that if it doesn't work out, "I'll just

give it away." "That won't be fair to the dog," I said. And this poor dog has an unhappy history to begin with. I rather wish that we were still not speaking, Mr. Willful and I. Kiss, kiss.

Their feud about her health did not end there. On July 11, three days before Larry was admitted to hospital, she emailed me asking my approval of an email she wanted to send to Larry to stop him who was still dishing her to their mutual friends.

> If I send the following e-mail to YFLT [Your Friend Larry Townsend], will it get you into trouble? No matter how many times you [Larry] say it—or how many people you [Larry] tell—I am not 80 years old, infirm and indigent. Repeating a lie does not make it so. Repeating a lie makes you [Larry] a Republican.

I immediately suggested she not send it:

> Please, in this instance, don't speak now; and forever hold your peace. Mark and I don't want to lose LT.... What do you care if he says you're 80; simply sometime drop to him that no matter what your age is he is eight years older.

Entering 2008, angry at everyone, with no Fred or Jeanne nearby to calm him, he informed me who lived over four-hundred miles away that he had hired a specifically lesbian attorney to sue bookstores and a publisher. He got hard threatening people with lawyers, and he was superstitious about lesbian super-powers getting what they want.

Fred was dead. Friends were at odds. He had no Fool from *King Lear* to warn him: "Thou shouldst not have been old till thou hadst been wise." Who would dare? Driven mad, he felt he was a man more sinned against than sinning, tearing down the narrative, the costumes, and the scenery of his life, business, and reputation.

All the pressures of a lifetime of homophobia and of shunning by literary establishment gatekeepers, steeped in the slow brew of his alcoholism, exploded into a grand finale of Hollywood rage with him swatting at planes like an aggrieved King Lear become an aggrieved King Kong fighting and falling in the final reel.

In the way that he had dumped exploitative publishers like Greenleaf Classics and Other Traveller thirty-five years before to protect his earliest copyrights, he lived his dying days explosive with anger pressing his scandalous lawsuit against dozens of small LGBT bookstores and Nazca Plains Publishing. He charged they had violated his copyrighted intellectual property by printing, distributing, and selling his books without authorization, and without paying royalties.

Feeling desperate, he wrote to Mark Hemry on April 27, 2008, asking him for help researching the copyrights for his books for which Larry could find no record. As a widower, he then posted, at the new website Mark created, a tender written profile, undercut with tincture of paranoia, that gave a distinct first-person self-defense account of his most difficult year personally, and most troubled year professionally, with alleged perfidious publishers like the unnamed Nazca Plains and with internet claim-jumpers who stole his name. This is the first posting that hinted at the coming brute force of his angry lawsuit. It is, as noted, very similar to that June 18, 1975, feature he wrote in *The Advocate*, declaring war on the Philadelphia gang of hoods violating his copyright.

> To my friends and fans, who have been so loyal and supportive during the most difficult period of my life. I want to thank everyone who has been there for me, most especially my good friends Jack Fritscher and Mark Hemry. These guys have gotten me started again, and back into some semblance of sanity. Mark, particularly, has been able to keep me going with his skill and knowledge of computers. Among other things, he has put this website together for me.
>
> As many of you know, I lost Fred, my friend and companion of 44 years, in July 2006. [How bittersweet those two nouns, *friend* and *companion*, so far from the sweeter *husband* and *spouse*.] At that time, I had already

decided to close down my mail-order business, but to continue writing. In keeping with this decision, I wrote a science-fiction novel, *TimeMasters*, which was accepted by a major gay publisher, who held it for two years, scheduled it for release in spring 2008, then sold out to another company which does not publish fiction. Again, with Mark's help, I intend to publish the story myself, and release it through this website. It is currently in production and I am already working on the sequel.

You probably noticed that [I have] a new web address....Unfortunately, during the months following Fred's death I had a few health issues of my own (now seemingly taken care of), and because of these distractions I apparently missed the renewal notice for my domain name, and someone highjacked it. So, unless and until I am able to recover my name, whatever you see offered or proposed under [site name]...has nothing to do with me.

There are also some unethical people in our community who saw an opportunity to exploit my byline, and even to republish some of my books without my permission. [Italics added] I think I have pretty well put a stop to this, but you may still see some web offerings that list a few of my titles as having been published by a company other than mine or by one of my legitimate, authorized publishers. As "they" say, "Shit happens."

His pulsating anger, the kind of arterial fury that pumped his heart, succeeded in freaking out the world of gay publishing.

Rachel Deahl summarized in mid-June the infamous lawsuit in *Publishers Weekly* which during years before had often generously reviewed his books like *Master's Counterpoints*.

A few weeks ago John Mitzel, proprietor of Calamus Books in Boston, was surprised to open his mail and discover he'd been named in a lawsuit filed by an author. The suit, filed by Larry Townsend's attorney for copyright infringement, stems from a dispute over unpaid fees allegedly owed the author by his distributor, the Oklahoma-based Nazca Plains Corp. Nonetheless, the suit charges that Mitzel, along with over 40 other booksellers (including Amazon and Barnes & Noble), infringed on Townsend's copyright by selling the author's books in his store.

As Larry's attack created fear nationwide, literary pioneer Deacon Maccubbin (b. 1940), the founding owner of Lambda Rising Bookstore (1974-2010) in Washington, D.C., and the founding publisher of *Lambda Book Report* and of the Lammy Awards, wrote a sensitive email inquiry on June 19, the day before my wedding:

> Subject: Jack, A bookseller's favor. I understand that you are close to Larry Townsend and I wonder if you might confidentially share with me his motivation in attacking so many of the remaining gay bookstores around the country, naming about 50 of them as co-defendants in his lawsuit against Herbert Moseley and Nazca Plains?
>
> ...Why on earth would he embroil gay bookstores in this battle? He seems to be determined to put all gay bookstores out of business, and might succeed even when losing his case, just due to the legal expense of defending ourselves against these frivolous and wholly unfounded charges. Does he really think that Lambda Rising, A Different Light, OutWrite Books, or Unabridged Books would ever knowingly or intentionally do anything to undermine a gay author, when we've devoted our whole existence to promoting and nurturing them? Something just does not compute here.
>
> One thing is certain, it's unlikely any bookstore in the country will ever be willing to return his books to their [display] shelves in light of this scorched earth lawsuit. I just can't imagine what his motivation might be. If you can shed any light on that (without violating any confidence or personal friendship), I would be most grateful.

This was a community crisis created by an author who got one rejection slip too many. Thinking he had been screwed by publishers and distributors and ignored by the gay literary establishment for his entire career, he set out to capture their amalgamated attention. The icon was tired of abuse, was cornered by death, and could not breathe.

Because I never wanted Larry's anger turned on me, I injected a wary bit of distance from him, and cautioned Mccubbin that I'd do what I could even though closeness to Larry was always relative.

I cannot emphasize too much that during the last lonely depressing months of his widower life, Larry and his two significants, Barney and Embry, were not speaking to one another. The trinity of their relationship was on life support. I seemed cast as the last writer-friend, the go-between, standing tangent to that circle of alienation speeding toward extinction. Was I, a San Franciscan, being swept away in LA? Were they playing me as I lay? As the audience for their grand finale? As their last eyewitness? Were we playing out *Tea and Sympathy* with its immortal line, one of the most famous final-curtain lines in gay theater history: "Years from now, when you talk about this, and you will, be kind." Even before Maccubbin's email, I had queried Jeanne about the *cause* of Larry's raging state of mind. She responded in a March 30, 2008, email about her revolving feud with him and his erratic behavior. She, who was in recovery, wrote:

> He continues to deny ever calling me a cunt...Speaking as an alcoholic, I can tell you that Larry is a textbook alcoholic.

And therein lies the tale.

24

**SUDDENLY THAT SUMMER:
JUNE AND JULY 2008
GAY MARRIAGE ON AND OFF AND ON AGAIN
TENNESSEE WILLIAMS, TOM OF FINLAND
TAXICAB CONFESSION
"I CAN'T BREATHE!"**

On May 15, 2008, the Supreme Court of California issued a decision legalizing same-sex marriage in California. It was to take effect on June 16. Suddenly that summer roared off to a grand start. Mark and I, together for twenty-nine years, planned our wedding for June 20 which was also my sixty-ninth birthday. Larry, who had no one to cuddle and comfort him, rejoiced with us saying again he wished he and Fred had been able to marry.

We knew the anti-gay clock was ticking on our human joy. The unforgivable Mormon Church in Utah immediately began occupying California politics. It interfered, and spent twenty million untaxed dollars to back California Proposition 8 which had been quickly written by Republicans to overturn gay marriage in the state. The anti-gay propaganda blitz succeeded. Gay marriage in California became illegal again on the day of the election, November 8, 2008—except for us 16,000 couples, 32,000 people, who managed to get hitched while the four-month window from June 16 to November 8 was open, and stay hitched by law when the U.S. Supreme Court overturned Proposition 8 on June 28, 2013.

That decision was five years after the fitful summer Larry, grieving Fred, died entangled in a public legal and social drama so stressful to his life and career that the lawsuit seemed almost a performative act of attempted suicide by the willful widower.

On May 25, 2008, for the Memorial Day holiday, Mark and I drove to Los Angeles for a working vacation to attend the annual Book Expo America at the LA Convention Center to debut my new book, and to visit with Larry and brunch with friends like Jeanne Barney, and my sometime writing partner David Hurles, the video artist Old Reliable, who weeks later would be permanently disabled with a drug-induced stroke after his ex-con hustler boyfriend betrayed him by moving a forty-six-year-old homeless female junkie off Santa Monica Boulevard into his apartment; and with pioneer archivist Durk Dehner and Steve Sharp of the Tom of Finland Foundation at 1421 Laveta Terrace in Echo Park; and with our beloved friend and collaborator Mark Thompson, former editor of *The Advocate*, and his soon-to be husband, Malcolm Boyd, the saintly Episcopalian beatnik coffeehouse priest and author of the 1965 bestseller, *Are You Running with Me, Jesus?*

Larry, author of the 1968 bestseller, *Run, Little Leather Boy*, could have associated himself with these diverse creative talents in the gay mainstream of LA, but he refused our invitation. They were a bit too arty and vanilla and queenstream for him to give them the time of day—especially because Thompson had dared exclude him from that 1992 anthology, *Leatherfolk*. He did, however, join us to stroll the BEA aisles where hundreds of publishers represented thousands of new books, including my *Gay San Francisco* to which Jeanne and Larry both contributed so much and for which Larry had written an "Introduction."

He was fretting personally because weeks before the BEA, he alleged he had invited an editor of the *Gay and Lesbian Review* to lunch so he could buy a display ad in the magazine; but, he said, the editor snubbed him and never called. He felt there was no end to the mainstream rejection of his kind of erotic gay pop culture. Everybody's sexual sadist was nobody's social masochist. He was mad as hell and wanted to sue all the bastards.

Distressed by his legal fight and estranged from his local friends, Larry welcomed any distraction and company who might levitate him from his own gravity of the kind that causes stars in the cosmos to collapse. Mark and I were staying in our usual suite at the Hotel California, a little gem, a surfer-themed hotel that made us feel young, at 1670 Ocean Avenue, one block south of the Santa Monica Pier. We liked the place because of the Eagles' album, *Hotel California*, which I quoted for the title of my memoir-novel, *Some Dance to Remember*. To swing his moods, we chatted up the hotel and its lost gay history as a diverting garden path to walk him down, calm him down, and nurture his flickering life force. He was a part of my life. He was winded and wounded. A quantum of solace, the amount of compassion one human can show for another, was owed him.

In terms of forgotten "Gay L. A." literary heritage and "Gay L. A." pop-culture walking tours, this Hotel California motor inn at 1670 Ocean Avenue was originally the palatial Hotel Arcadia and Bath House (1887-1904), then the transient Langdon Hotel during the desperate wartime housing shortage (1940s), and is now—since 2019, after years as the Hotel California—the surfer-tourist Sea Blue Hotel. This Santa Monica inn is the "End of the Trail," the last stop on the fabled "Route 66" of novelists John (*Grapes of Wrath*) Steinbeck and Jack (*On the Road*) Kerouac and of the Eagles' hitchhiking song "Standin' on the Corner in Winslow, Arizona." This "Main Street of America," documented in Bobby Troup's famous travelog song "Get Your Kicks on Route 66," begins its storied road trip in Chicago, stretches 2500 miles of straight and gay cruising and no-tell motels, and finally dead-ends literally in the Tongva Park public sculpture across the street from the Sea Blue Hotel front door and its gay history.

The inn itself sits at the top of the Arcadia Terrace Steps (1911) which lead down to Appian Way and the original Muscle Beach built by the WPA in 1934. Before Muscle Beach was forced to move to Venice Beach in 1959—because outraged local puritans loathed its liberated sex appeal and queer presence—that world-famous outdoor gym-platform in the sand by the Santa Monica Pier was for years a gay magnet for sex tourists. It pulled Larry and midcentury gay men with cars, cash, and cameras to the pop-up gayborhood to admire the unemployed and nearly naked gymnasts, bodybuilders, muscleman bikers, and Hollywood stuntmen who often rented by the hour.

As a quintessential gay space, Muscle Beach was a recruiting station for photographers who focused the gay gaze to create the beefcake fetish of the iconic blond California Look: "Bruce of LA" who influenced Herb Ritts and Robert Mapplethorpe; Bob Mizer in his AMG studios' *Physique Pictorial* magazine who influenced Larry; and Jim French who could not resist moving his Colt Studio from New York to LA. Muscle Beach is so iconic in gay culture that Larry's friend, Tom of Finland, immigrated from Finland to LA to draw his platonic ideals of blond leather muscle. Among Larry's peerage of gay pulp-fiction authors, he was aware that half a dozen pulp novels featured the words *Muscle Beach* in their titles like Guild Press' *The Boys of Muscle Beach* (1969).

I told Larry that during the wartime summer of 1943 when racist white servicemen on leave in LA started the anti-Latino "Zoot Suit" race riots, Tennessee Williams, who championed Hispanic culture in his plays, cruised down the stairs daily to Muscle Beach through the grounds and victory garden of the Langdon when he lived just one minute across the street at 1647 Ocean Avenue. His crowded rooming house was next to the Dawn Hotel which, remodeled in 1959, became one of Larry's favorite restaurants, Chez Jay, at 1657 Ocean Avenue. Larry admitted that after dining *Chez Jay*, he sometimes cruised the Arcadia Steps as a *digestif* until he met Fred in 1963.

Trying anything to buck up the depressed Larry, I told him that Tennessee while writing a Lana Turner picture at MGM fought with the moguls—the way Larry himself fought with publishers—and kept on with his creative life sitting out his contract living *la dolce vita* on the beach while drafting *The Glass Menagerie* and drawing 250 dollars a week. (In 1996, encouraging Larry even then to lighten up and look at himself, I titled my introduction to his *Leatherman's Handbook*, 25th-Anniversary Edition, as "Leather Dolce Vita, Pop Culture, and the Prime of Mr. Larry Townsend.")

I tried to humor him, telling him Tennessee hired civilian trade and U.S. servicemen lounging on the Arcadia Steps the way his Mrs. Stone solicited Roman hustlers draped across the Spanish Steps. Showing him around the gardens of our hotel, I tried to raise his spirits to keep him creating despite adversity. I told him how the prolific Tennessee had made these local gardens into the detailed gardens featured in his short story "The Mattress by the Tomato Patch," which he drafted on this spot in 1943 while sitting in the very gardens which he described in recognizeable detail long before the Langdon became the Hotel California.

Larry half-listened to my literary cheerleading about the local color of this lost gayborhood and the 1940s gay-roots importance of Tennessee Williams to leather culture. I wanted him aware and proud and grateful that in creating Stanley and casting Brando in *A Streetcar Named Desire* in 1947, Williams revved up the 1950s pop-culture archetype of the intensely masculine post-war blue-collar rebel bikers in leather who were Larry's bread and butter. I didn't tell him that Tennessee wrote better S&M stories than he did, like "One Arm" and "Desire and the Black Masseur."

Literature offers vicarious and cautionary experiences about coping with life, but Larry, who was not an intellectual all-rounder, did not read or learn from literature—unless he was looking for a property he could adapt. I didn't dare tell him about Tennessee's poem "Mad at Night." It opens: "Old men go mad at night / but are not Lears." It ends: "And old men have no Fools except themselves." Why should he be interested in leftover bits from my 1966 doctoral dissertation on Williams who like Larry died writing and fighting to survive?

He was way more fixated on schooling us two driving around for hours in the back seats of his Cadillac Escalade while he told us the history of his life. The act of driving seemed to hypnotize him. He had never before been so open. Those five days of rides were a moving confessional of Hollywood flashbacks as he drove us down LA streets streaming past straight and gay addresses that triggered his nostalgia. We knew what was going on. He was like an old taxi driver spilling his life story to the last passengers he would ever have. His monologue was casual with personal detail. Trained in the Catholic seminary to hear confessions, I made mental notes because I did not want to take out pen and paper and make him self-conscious. His taxicab confession was the candid interview everyone wanted from The Townsend, and its free associations infuse this memoir.

In 1992, Bob Wingate, the publisher of *Bound & Gagged* magazine, met Larry for the first time, through LA video director Bob Jones whose young "S&M punk" sex tapes Larry sold mail-order for years until they argued and had a falling out. Jones, pointing out Larry's constant dyspepsia, told Wingate that "Larry was disgruntled that, for all his fame, no one had ever actually done an interview with him." Wingate said:

> I told Larry I'd be happy to interview him for *Bound & Gagged*, though *B&G* had never been an interview-style publication. I did the interview, and several months after it was published, Larry started writing a regular column for *Bound & Gagged*, which continued until we ceased publication in June, 2005.

Wingate's clever cover copy proclaimed Larry's marquee name: "*Bound and Gagged*, January/February, 1993. Issue 32; 'Carnivores & Vegetarians in Bondage Frenzy' PLUS Larry Townsend Grants First Interview!"

25

LAST BRUNCH AT CASA DEL MAR
SANTA MONICA
JUNE 1, 2008

On Sunday, June 1, 2008, in the fifth-last week before Larry collapsed into two unconscious weeks in Intensive Care, Mark and I walked down the strand of sandy beach from the Santa Monica Pier and the Hotel California to the Hotel Casa del Mar where the Navy housed enlisted sailors during the World War. It was there Larry met us for brunch and introduced his friend Derrick who was a quiet older man and avid hiker who would soon on July 13 drive the dying Larry the three miles from his home to Cedars-Sinai Hospital Emergency, two miles from the French Quarter restaurant. Larry tried to be congratulatory that my gay history book—much of which was, because of his and Jeanne's contributions, about him and her as well as their pals Embry, Legrand, and Earl—had won a ForeWord Small Press Best LGBT Nonfiction Award at the BEA. It ticked him a bit because he felt the ForeWord Award had a certain out-of-the-ghetto cachet he envied in that its discernment came, he judged, not from the usual gay-award circuit party of vested comrades, consorts, and cronies, but from independent critics, staff, and judges at a straight literary magazine.

If it was jealousy of the kind slapped out by his circle of French Quarter accomplices, he, with his own several book awards, was trying to be very careful to tamp that emotion down because his long list of friends had become a short list, and he didn't want to lose his brokered link to Jeanne. He ought to have been pleased because he and she and I for the previous two years had been close with our heads together about the oral-history content of my book.

At that brunch on the last day of the BEA, a mere seven street miles from the French Quarter, he could not help but grumble and stew about his lawsuit. Because he again asked our opinion, we both urged him, perhaps too politely in front of his friend, to stop the suit because it would destroy his reputation.

The "S&M High Priest" listened, staring out the big glass windows at the ocean, like the defeated and defrocked fallen priest in *Night of the Iguana* contemplating a long final swim to China, and said nothing. So we changed the subject and reminded him we were to be married on June 20. It brought a smile back to his face, and, as our little procession left the restaurant, we took pictures of each other standing on the grand staircase at Casa del Mar.

We did not know we were witnessing the Passion and Death of Larry Townsend. None of us knew then that we would never see each other again, and I'm glad we hugged and kissed goodbye.

On June 8, I wrote to Jeanne:

> Larry called today to make sure he was still in our good graces after ignoring the book award....He wants us to design his books and promote him [in contests]...and yet he himself rarely bothers to enter contests because he thinks he's either beyond competing, or that he might not win, when the irony is he actually could win if he would organize himself....I fear he will be very sorry for naming all the bookstores as defendants in his vainglorious lawsuit against Herbert at Nazca Plains Publishing. For pennies, and for revenge, he risks losing the good will of book buyers in the ever-shrinking world of gay bookstores. It is a kind of King Lear Madness, but I cannot deliver him from his diktats about how the world is shit.

On June 13, back in Northern California a week before our wedding, a pickup truck crashed T-bone into Mark and me in our parked Volvo precisely next to the seatbelt strapped over my right shoulder. It was like a small bomb went off. Glass blew everywhere. Mark, in his seatbelt, was thrown against the steering wheel, but unhurt. I was trapped inside the car by the smashed door, and almost instantly, a dreamy young fireman reaching in through the window was holding my dazed head and telling me to stop moving, and I said, "I can't surrender," and he held my face tight in his hands, and said, "No one likes to give up control."

Holding my head steady, he asked an old question that suddenly that summer had a very new answer. Pointing at Mark, he said, "Who's he to you?" I said, "My husband." He said, "Cool."

And he pulled me out the window of the wreckage and sent me off with EMTs in an ambulance. What wedding doesn't have its ups and downs? The accident triggered Jeanne and Larry's feelings. That day, she wrote: "I love you both so very much." For our June 20 wedding, Larry sent us grooms a bouquet of fifty red roses.

He must have enjoyed our previous visit, because on June 25, he invited us to please drive back to LA to go with him to the 4th of July Car Show he attended annually in Santa Barbara, but we were still too shaken by the accident to drive so soon on freeways. He went anyway, with Derrick, and came home complaining he couldn't breathe.

On June 27, Jeanne, stressed by her own illness, penned a sad picture of the self-disappearing "Daughter of the Elephant Girl" whose wilting and withering worried Larry, the "Son of a Spy," who felt his "leather wife" was a mirror of his own decline. She wrote to me:

> Incidentally, this is apt to be my last communication for awhile. I am in severe pain about 50% of the time; merely uncomfortable the other 50%, and deeply depressed... about the state of the country/world all the time. I simply have no energy. [She could not be there for him, nor he for her.] I am having the same problem with my right arm as my left. Plus, those crippling headaches have been coming out of nowhere, for no apparent reason, and laying me low for up to 36 hours....Before my spine collapsed and my leg died, I was able to wear four-to-five-inch heels...now, of course, [wearing them] I would look like a troll.

Like Didion characters, they were a done, done, and undone Los Angeles couple divorcing while straddling fault lines at the end of things.

Jeanne mused:

> I increasingly think of my mother's last weeks and the comment of the hospice workers about "Failure to Thrive." I find myself slipping into that place and must fight very hard to stay away. This requires making some major changes as I am able.

That same day I responded to her and mentioned how our suitcases were packed because north of San Francisco we were on notice to be ready to evacuate because of the worsening climate firestorm raging in the forests near our home, and that we were hoping the air would be clear and clean enough for the San Francisco Pride Parade, celebrating gay marriage, the following Sunday.

On June 28, Larry emailed good wishes, and distress:

> Jack. Just got the new *Gay San Francisco* book. It looks great. (Do you know this is the first time we have been under the covers together?) Other news: After 25 years, *Honcho* is dropping my column. Claim they can't afford to pay me. Ah, well, that's the way of it. Durk [Dehner] should send out the press release [publicizing supportive news of the lawsuit]. So far, no response from that a-hole [publisher] in TX. [And then he mentioned his latest disability impacting his writing.] My hands are worse than ever, but fortunately the voice recognition software is working. [He closed on a love note of affection.] Hope you are both recovering from the after-effects of the accident, the excitement of your marriage, life in general. All best wishes to you both. Love, Larry

It was sad to be a witness to the their suffering, and to their competition in the crying game. Because their distress continued to distress me, Mark reassured it was okay that these suffering elders, this estranged Hollywood couple, was using me as a plot device, a go-between, as in "Tell your friend LT." Jeanne's emails to me were really emails to Larry. It helped that she and he were gracious about my stenography of their words. Jeanne gave enthusiastic permission to quote her in my books. She wrote, "Quote me! Quote me!" about sharing her emails and thirty hours of taped conversations. Two years earlier when I was researching and writing *Gay San Francisco: Eyewitness Drummer*, I had asked her for her personal experiences around leather life in Los Angeles, and she, a woman scorned and still smarting from her erasure by Faderman and Timmons' in *Gay L.A.*, wrote on September 5, 2006: "As for an eyewitness, that would be me."

26

THE EMAIL LETTER: DROP THAT LAWSUIT!
A TIMELINE OF DECLINE
DYING IN PLAIN SIGHT

Responding immediately to Larry's distressed June 28 email, I wrote him insisting he drop the lawsuit. Because we had bonded so sweetly those confessional nights in his Escalade, I wrote as tactfully as I could because I risked losing a most interesting friend whose alpha intransigence I tried to break with insistent repetition:

> Dear Larry, So happy to be under the covers again with you. Actually, we were under the covers together twelve years ago when you asked me to write an introduction to the "Silver Anniversary Edition" of your first *Leatherman's Handbook*. What fun! I'm always so happy to be together anywhere with you.
>
> If I may suggest, and if *Honcho* is willing to do it, presuming you are willing to do it, make a deal with them to continue writing your monthly column—minus a paycheck—in trade for a free sixth-page ad (that costs them nothing) for your mail-order books. However, *Honcho* probably wants to move on into the future, and that leaves old fucks like you and me (nothing personal but we are both so last midcentury) out of the new DNA of the changing leather LGBT picture.
>
> I don't wish to piss you off, so don't get mad at me, but from all the feedback I've heard about your attorney suing the bookstores, perhaps the only press release you [aided by Durk Dehner] should do is to advise bookstores

you are dropping them from this case which is about Nazca Plains only.

Think of it: bookstores may never order a single more copy of an LT book because there is no way for them to know that it is a legit copy.

The word is that your attorney has gone too far. If you never listen to me again, listen to this: drop the bookstore suit, have your attorney back off the bookstores, and send out a PR notice about that news.

I can tell you for sure that you will destroy your career in bookstores. I am hearing things that you will never hear as the person suing these people. What I'm telling you here, frankly, dear Larry, because I love you, is that you are also doing yourself damage in dollars if your attorney does not back off and APOLOGIZE to the innocent bookstores who have enough troubles.

Don't let your righteous take on Nazca ruin your years-long relationship with bookstores. If that happens, Herbert wins.

You win if bookstores continue to carry your books, and I, to tell you the truth, my dear friend, have been told in these last two weeks (by bookstore owners) that if you continue this pursuit of the bookstores you will be blacklisted by them, and at our age, with so little time left, that is not a good thing.

I want you to be remembered as the good and gracious Larry Townsend, and not as the "bitter and senile old man" cliché which some bookstores are beginning to use to diminish and define you. You deserve better.

I don't want you ever to become angry with me, but... the bookstores see this suit as the kiss of death for you.

Dude, don't let your career end this way. Have the lesbian attorney back off NOW TODAY and send a letter NOW TODAY dropping the suit against the stores. You and Durk Dehner might send out a conciliatory, if not apologetic, press release that will save you and your wonderful lifetime's work from this terrible backlash.

I beg you not to get angry with me. I beg you to listen....Everyone thinks we have been *Brokeback* since 1970. Actually, the bookstore owners like you very much, and they are appalled at this turn of events, and they want to know what the fuck is going on with you. Don't even think about this; just do it. Stop the suit against the few bookstores that remain in business. They may not be all that great, but they are all you have because you have so banked on LGBT bookstores over the years.

I wish your hands were better, and we are both happy your voice recognition is working. Let the bookstores hear that same cheery LT voice they have heard over the years.

Thanks for asking. We are both okay after the horrible accident, although we still do not have our Volvo back which is a problem because tomorrow we want to drive into San Francisco for the Gay Pride Parade to march with its first honeymoon contingent of married couples.

As your friend, I must tell you: you have no choice. You MUST drop this suit against bookstores IMMEDIATELY and get word to the bookstores ASAP.

Call if you have any questions. Love, Jack and Mark

On June 30, Larry and I discussed the lawsuit in a 45-minute telephone conversation. That same day, Durk Dehner sent Larry's attorney a press release from the Tom of Finland Foundation supporting the lawsuit.

On July 2, Larry wrote:

Jock [He often called me "Jock" or "Herr Doktor Fritscher"], If you will tell me which bookstores you have heard from specifically, I'll make sure [my attorney] drops them. I'm meeting with her next week...Thanks, Larry.

In a telephone call on July 5, I told him again, when he asked again, to drop Lambda Rising Bookstore as well as all the other small bookstores. It was a friendly call and it was the last time Larry and I spoke before he died.

On July 9, with him having only four days of consciousness left, I wrote:

> Dear Larry, I'm sorry to be caught in the middle of "The Case of the Publisher-Bookstore-Author"....I hope it's not a no-win situation. In response to your email request to assist you, I have taken the time since to query some of those involved. However, in the same way that you told me you can't be in touch with the bookstores because of the plaintiff-defendant relationship, the bookstores don't wish at this time to be in touch with you either. It would be easier for me to skate a Figure 8 on an ice cube. Other than what I wrote to you in my long email, there seems to be nothing else I can do. Believe me, Mark and I are in your corner about Nazca and wish that Herbert had never [allegedly] done you wrong. Mark and I are a team of a couple who are always both here for you. We hope this all works out for you...

On July 12, leather historian Boi Gwen Hardy wrote from Florida thanking me for answering her request to write a thousand-word toast-and-roast biography for Jeanne to be read to the audience when La Barney received a Lifetime Achievement Award at the Pantheon of Leather Weekend in Chicago, July 18 to 20. Vi Johnson, founder of the Carter/Johnson Leather Library, had nominated Jeanne for the award granted by Pantheon owner Dave Rhodes who wrote me: "I respected and learned from Larry. He self-published, cutting out the huge and expensive middlemen."

Needless to say, the springtime announcement of Jeanne's Lifetime Award added to the royal rumble that summer between Jeanne and Larry who reminded her he had received his own Pantheon Lifetime Achievement Award thirteen years earlier.

27

THE PASSION AND DEATH OF
LARRY TOWNSEND
"PERHAPS YOU CAN SAVE HIS LIFE
AS YOU SAVED HIS REPUTATION"

On July 13, Jeanne sent me an email mourning the death of her favorite fashion model Dorian Leigh who was the sister of my favorite fashion model/actress, Suzy Parker, who had died in 2003. Unknown to us, that same summer day, Larry was suddenly admitted to Cedars-Sinai Hospital Emergency where he was immediately sedated and intubated and never regained consciousness.

On July 14, a biopsy was done on his lungs. I remembered that in 2006, a couple of months before Fred died, Larry had a severe lung infection. He, who was never a smoker of anything, kept telling me, the way the worried obsess over symptoms, that after his return from the car show in Santa Barbara where the air was polluted with climate-fire smoke, he was so short of breath he could hardly walk through his house.

On July 18, Roger Earl and Terry Legrand called me saying Larry was not answering his phone, and they were worried. I wrote to Jeanne:

> Guys on the gay grapevine have contacted me asking for verification and updates on the news that Larry is in the hospital and his condition is surmised to be caused by the stress of the lawsuit. None of this may be true. Have you heard anything? Mark and I have called both his numbers, but no answer.

Jeanne responded July 19:

As you know, he no longer speaks to me. And the list of contacts I had from his last hospitalization was tossed out some time ago. However, I do have a number for his friend Derrick. This [possible hospitalization] would be terribly inconvenient for me.

Earlier this morning, and at great personal cost, I dragged many pounds of his stuff [his books which she sold mail-order] to the front of the house so that I could drag it all to the porch tomorrow. I was going to notify him that it could be picked up when [her sharpened fingernails typed with Initial Capital Letters] he does his usual Sunday Gala Brunch with The New Fred.

Of course, this [hospitalization] might explain why I've had no response to my email asking for an email address for his Gestapo officer [his assistant who was to pick up the goods].

Please let me know what, if anything, you find out so that I can drag this shit away from my front door.

On the morning of July 20, the morning of the day Jeanne was to receive her Lifetime Achievement Award, she wrote she could find out nothing about Larry:

Any news about YFLT? It occurred to me that he'd been talking about having some varicose veins taken care of.

I responded twenty minutes later forwarding the sudden, awful, heart-breaking news I'd just received from Larry's family:

Dear Jeanne, News. Larry had asked Mark and me to drive down to Santa Barbara to go with him to a car show on the 4th of July. We couldn't because of our car crash, but he went as planned although he was having a problem with shortness of breath. His doctor thought it was stress. By the time he returned from Santa Barbara—remember all the smoke in the air from the 1000 fires—he was so short of breath he could hardly go from room to room. He had had a lung infection some years ago and the meds from that had caused a cataract. So he went to or was taken to Cedars-Sinai where on July 14 a biopsy was done on his lung and there is as yet no word on that tissue sample. He has a tube down his throat and is heavily sedated and cannot speak because of the tube. The sedation is being lessened each day, and his sister who has been with him this last week will probably return to Northern California today. I'll let you know more as soon as I know more.

An hour later, I wrote:

Mark and I just tried to send Larry a bouquet, but the Cedars-Sinai floral shop, which has always been so helpful in the past, said he could not have flowers because he is in ICU.

On July 22, Jeanne wrote:

Jack, dear— When you called at 9 p.m. on Sunday, I could feel a killer headache coming on. All day yesterday I was in bed, in the dark, with my head packed in ice. That is, "in bed," when I wasn't up falling down, throwing up, feeding the animals. Obviously, I am up now—still severe head pain, still severe neck pain, still dizzy—but no more falling down, throwing up. I guess that's progress.

When Gwen called on Sunday at 3 p.m., she passed on the news about YFLT.

I don't understand why he wanted you two to drive down to Santa Barbara. He goes to that car show with his barber and his barber's partner; they drive up in a classic car, which they enter in the show. I can't imagine his going to that alone. He doesn't even go to lunch or the movies by himself.

But if I could figure him out—well...
Cheers, Jeanne

On July 24, Boi Gwen wrote that my Lifetime Achievement profile of Jeanne had surprised Gwen's leather friends at Pantheon who told her that "they were quite shocked at what Jeanne had accomplished." Most were from a younger generation, she said, "who never knew who Jeanne was until they heard your bio on her."

Then came the humbling of any and every one of us whoever thought we were something gay and grand at the French Quarter: "To be quite honest," she added, "I'm not even sure they know who you are, or what you have done in our leather history past."

This invisibility is the de-powering of identity that happens when mainstream queer history scholarship, like the loud gay silence in *Gay L.A.*, excludes leatherfolk from gay American history.

She concluded: "I put it out on the 'Leather Titleholders List' that Larry was in the hospital and asked everyone to keep him in their leather prayers."

On that same day, Sam Streit responded to my email telling him Larry was *in extremis*:

> Dear Jack, I am so sorry to hear this, and really very surprised. Larry sent me a copy of his new book, with a note, just a couple of weeks ago and in the note he said he would call me soon. I had kept the note on my desk rather than in his file to remind myself that if he didn't call reasonably soon I should give him a call. He and I had a number of phone conversations (he doesn't like email very much, as you know) and I sent him, at his request, a copy of John Preston's will so that he could have his attorney draw up a similar bequest intention. I don't know that he did so.

By Friday, July 25, the international gay-community chatter reported incorrectly that Larry had suffered a heart attack. Deacon Maccubbin, circling through the rumors with his good sense of gallows humor, sent me the best news ever at 1:28 PM. Just hours before Larry collapsed with no time to start spreading the news, he had capitulated on the lawsuit; and while he was in ICU, his attorney had quietly followed his directive. Deacon wrote:

Larry Townsend dropped us and about a dozen other bookstores from his lawsuit, though there are still a number of stores named. In the meantime, Larry apparently had a stroke and is rumored to be in critical condition in the hospital. Meanwhile, [famous name deleted] stepped in [to] a public forum on the web, and allegedly made death threats against the distributor [publisher] who was the prime target of Larry's suit.

Somebody needs to start typing!

This would make a great soap opera!

Because Durk Dehner was such a passionate art professional who had jumped to Larry's defense in his lawsuit, I emailed him that same day to tell him the bad news of Larry's collapse.

Dear Durk. The next 72 to 96 hours are crucial. As Tuesday July 29 approaches, when a life-and-death decision must be made, please remember Larry and his family in your thoughts, prayers, and good energy.

Durk, who was in Europe defending Tom of Finland's copyrights, immediately responded:

Jack. it is Saturday here in The Netherlands and I feel so involved with this as it was the [Tom of Finland] Foundation that did the press release on the lawsuit against Moseley, and then I had to leave the country and its been one month and I haven't returned as of yet. Please give me the contact information for whoever is in charge of his medical so I can contact them. I am sure I can be of use in this situation, and I know what I can say to him even if he is sedated. I will come home as soon as possible. Please send me your phone number so I can reach you.... Durk

On July 26, I emailed:

Dear Jeanne, Larry continues to lie ventilated in ICU in an induced deep sleep, and he seems comfortable. A filter has been inserted in his leg to catch any blood clot before it travels up to the torso. This allows a reduction of the blood-thinning medicine he was being given. All his family will be present on Sunday for a Monday consultation with the doctors because Tuesday [under his living will] is the fourteenth day of his sedation, and that is a milestone in consideration of his present state and his further treatment. Honestly, it seems that he is leaving us.

Thankfully, one great thing he did this month was that, after that June 28 email I wrote to him which I copied to you, Larry did, in fact, drop his lawsuit against Lambda Rising bookstore and other small bookstores; he narrowed the focus to Nazca Plains. He actually was working his way into handling and focusing the stress and betrayal and chagrin he felt when the copyrights to his books were violated.

Larry has always been such a thunderous presence, moving like a storm-front blowing across the social and literary landscape, that it seems impossible that he now lies quiet.

Because he always stood up for himself, and because you sometimes accompanied him to the opera, and because he loves Puccini, you can understand that as his time comes I hope that his family puts headphones on him and plays "Nessun Dorma."

"Nobody shall sleep!...Nobody shall sleep! / Even you, oh Prince, / In your cold room, watch the stars / ... [If] we must, alas, die. Vanish, oh Night! Set, stars! Set, stars! / At dawn, / I will win! I will win! I will win!"

As ever, Jack and Mark

On Sunday, July 27, I wrote to a dozen leatherfolk on the email tree:

Our friend Larry Townsend remains in ICU where he has been since July 13. Contrary to internet rumors, he has not had a heart attack. Larry has pneumonia and is deeply sedated on a ventilator, and he has other complications. I am in constant contact with his family. The next 72 hours are crucial. As Tuesday July 29 approaches, please remember Larry and his family in your thoughts, prayers, and good energy. July 29 will be two years and three weeks since Larry's longtime partner Fred died.

On July 28, I updated Jeanne:

Larry remains deeply sedated because of the breathing tube, and the good news is he's breathing more on his own, and his eyes are open. Tomorrow is the end of the two-week window on the respirator. I figured out a couple of days ago that Larry went into the hospital on July 13 exactly two years and five days after Fred died.

In as much as you mention my email that caused Larry to change his mind about suing the bookstores, Mark wanted me to mention that the email you sent to Larry (without meaning to, you said) in which you chastised his stormy behavior actually did a lot of good. Immediately after he received it, we noticed his attitude to us, and to the world, was suddenly sweeter and kinder. So, kiddo, ya done good. Love, J&M

Luckily, for once, he who listened to no one, listened—and saved his bruised leather soul. In the last week of his conscious life, he made that *mea culpa* decision because he realized the bookstores were not part of his alleged problem with the publisher. The lawsuit itself nevertheless exhibited something positive about his lifelong mission to protect gay writers and their copyrights that he began in earnest in San Francisco on June 15, 1970, at that first Gay Writers Conference at the SIR Center for the Society for Individual Rights. Of all the gay rights he championed, his passion was to alert LGBT creators not to be so masochistic that they sign over their copyrights to publishers in order to have their writing, drawings, and photographs make it into print.

On July 28, Deacon Maccubbin responded kindly to the email sent him the day before, in which I asked:

Please do not think ill of Larry [for suing you]. He is a recent widower who has been in failing health the last year. In the end, he has listened to reason.

Deacon wrote:

Thank you so much for your report on Larry Townsend's health, as well as for the background on his change of heart regarding the lawsuit. I will be thinking positive thoughts of Larry today and hoping for his recovery.

Lambda Rising and the other glbt bookstores that were dropped from the suit are in your debt for the efforts you made on our behalf.

Is it okay with you if I share your report (either as you wrote it, or paraphrased) with the other bookstores affected? I'm sure they would want to know how this all came about.

I responded:

Hi, Deacon, Thanks. Yes, you have my permission to share my email with the bookstores. Everything about this ongoing lawsuit is of public concern to the entire LGBT community. Larry remains alive, and where there is life there is the cliché of hope...Having done what I could to address your request, and, considering that Larry now lies *in extremis*, I was able to act just in the nick of time.

It was fortunate that you queried me when you did twenty-three days before his collapse. It gave some time to maneuver through my honeymoon joys, and his stress and chagrin, and the disappointment he felt when his copyrights were violated.

If my personal efforts have helped save Lambda Rising and other bookstores from being sued, I am very happy that I was able to act in your defense.

During the days Larry lay unconscious in Intensive Care, Jeanne emailed twice asking for news. On July 27, she wrote:

Perhaps you can save his life as you saved his reputation?

On July 29, at 7:23 AM, eight hours before Larry passed, Durk Dehner returning from Amsterdam texted me praising Larry's crusading courage:

> I got a hold of larry's family on their way to the hospital this morning to do the deed of pulling his life support. I asked them to give me an opportunity to speak with him for one last try...it aint over til it is and maybe they will call me back. it saddens me greatly for we need people like larry townsend who is the queer larry flynt in some regards as in ethics. [Larry Flynt (1942-2021) founded *Hustler* magazine in 1974, lived in the Hollywood Hills near Larry and Fred, and crusaded for freedom of the press.] he is one who is willing to be unliked by those of short-sightedness for he sees the importance of standing up to thugs who take advantage and abuse the naive vulnerable creative beings in our community. I do want him to be around for this fight with herbert moseley. durk

Larry died, unforgettably for me, on my deceased father's birthday, July 29. On July 31, I received an email from Nazca Plains publisher Herbert Moseley who himself was perhaps an innocent who happened to be in the wrong place when Larry began raging against death by threatening some kind of cosmic legal vengeance, as did Embry, against anyone he figured had done 'im wrong. Herbert wrote:

> We have been following your very sensitive postings about the illness and passing of Larry Townsend. We join with the many others who thought Larry was one of the most gifted and prolific gay writers. It is regretful that the lawsuit was filed against so many bookstores and others who were trying to continue to proliferate Larry's messages...Perhaps because of his illness, Larry got involved with...an attorney who seems to be much more interested in collecting her own legal fees...Nazca Plains Corporation has never sought to hurt Larry, but

that seems irrelevant to [his attorney. He then added the kicker.] I wonder whether you would be kind enough to provide a back channel for Nazca Plains to try and settle the matter with the family...

Moseley's plan would have flooded the market with a devalued dump of Larry's remaindered books. He wrote:

> As an aside, our plan is to donate, on behalf of Larry's heirs, the thousands of authorized [*sic*] and contracted [*sic*] books in our warehouse to the Leather Museum [Leather Archives & Museum of Chicago] who could issue a tax receipt that the family could then use as a deduction against probate taxes... If you can believe [Larry's attorney], she claims to have learned of Larry's death for the first time from reading your column.

I washed my hands of the case. My concern had been for Larry himself, and then for the bookstores, in the misbegotten lawsuit in which everyone involved, including the attorney, was probably an innocent bystander caught up in his frustration about his lifelong exclusion from the gay mainstream.

I wasn't going to ask what makes people misbehave, or seem evil, as Joan Didion ruminated in her first line in *Play It as It Lays*: "What makes Iago evil? Some people ask. I never ask."

Maybe the fighting frenemies brunching at the French Quarter were all swept away by something weird in LA—something raw in the blistering Santa Ana desert winds that every autumn blow down from the eastern mountains, west across LA, and make locals go mental sitting isolated in their cars on the 405 threading bumper-to-bumper through the slow tangle of the smoky freeways as the dry Santa Anas set the hills around LA on fire.

On August 20, 2008, a month after Larry passed, his family invited Mark and me to his home in Los Angeles to help begin to identify and sort his archive of writing, art, and photography which we did finally around the dining-room table of his niece's home in Berkeley. In 2012, Carole Queen, founder of the San Francisco Center for Sex & Culture blogged, "We are so grateful to have been gifted with [some of] Townsend's archives." Queen's

Center then exhibited its own version of his BDSM archives featuring "personal ephemera including toys, leathers, and original manuscripts."

28

FROM THE *DRUMMER* SALON TO *HONCHO*

Larry Townsend's signature "Leather Notebook" advice column appeared in *Drummer* for twelve years from 1980 to 1992. When he exited *Drummer*, he re-titled his column "Ask Larry" and sold it to *Honcho* where it was published for thirteen years until canceled, June 26, 2008, thirty-three days before his death, in a sensitive email from *Honcho* editor Gordon Wallace:

> Hi, Larry—hope you are doing well. To my dismay, I have had drastic budget cuts imposed on my titles. Consequently, I will be unable to continue with your column. (I know reimbursement for the column is low, but even that amount cannot be accommodated given the new budget.) The last paid column will need to be for the *Honcho* January '09 issue which is due July 5. [Hailing Larry's iconic status, Gordon finished kindly.] I do recognize that your column brings something special to the magazine, and that it is something of an "institution" in the magazine. I really do appreciate your contribution, and I am sorry to break this news.

After Larry's family asked me to send *Honcho* my first short obituary, it was published as a valedictory salute in February 2009, and *Honcho* itself died a few months later.

29

A MONTAGE RECAP
A KING TUT SARCOPHAGUS IN THE TV ROOM
AN EARTHQUAKE
"A SHOCKING REVELATION
FROM TOM OF FINLAND"

In a final summary montage of the Great Man, Larry Townsend's last novel *TimeMasters* was published in April 2008, a hundred days before his death. His last published writing was his "Introduction" to *Gay San Francisco: Eyewitness Drummer—A Memoir of the Sex, Art, and Salon of Drummer Magazine 1975-1999*. His lover of forty-three years, Fred Yerkes, died two years before him on July 7, 2006, succumbing alone late at night while watching television. Larry, waking in the night and missing him in bed, found him just before dawn lying peacefully on the big leather couch that sat next to their six-foot-tall King Tut sarcophagus. The colorful coffin stood upright in the corner of the screening room they had furnished with dozens of Tut knickknacks from the Franklin Mint. Both Larry and Fred, like many gay men, had been deeply touched by the traveling "Treasures of Tutankhamun" exhibit that set records for museum attendance in 1978. When gay marriage became legal in California on June 16, 2008, six weeks before Larry died, he wrote to Mark and me the constant refrain he had voiced earlier that month while we were cruising around LA in that gas-guzzling Cadillac Escalade whose luxury he loved:

> I'd like to have someone to marry. Fred and I would have been married. Thank God, though, for the domestic-partner law because it saved me so much trouble when Fred died.

Four weeks after celebrating the publication of *TimeMasters*, he lay unconscious in Cedars-Sinai ICU. Two weeks later, without regaining consciousness and surrounded by his family, he died, about fifteen minutes after he was taken off life support.

At his own request, he was cremated by the Neptune Society with no funeral or memorial service. Nevertheless, Durk Dehner, true to the end, hosted a wake for him at the Tom of Finland Foundation at 2 PM, Sunday, September 7. It was attended by intimates Jeanne Barney, Terry Legrand, Roger Earl, and a few other friends.

Did Durk's written invitation to a last hurrah reveal Larry's shocking and bitter prank against the literary establishment that may have been, rather than a prank, a desperate plea for attention by an old man who was grieving the loss of his spouse, his career, and his life?

Durk wrote a punch line worthy of a stealth-narrator in *Play It as It Lays*. It shocked me even as it confirmed the Townsend temperament I knew so well. Does he who laughs last, really laugh best?

Durk wrote:

> *Larry never intended to pursue the suit with the bookstores; he just wanted them to vent their anger on Moseley—the one who was truly responsible.* [Italics added for emphasis]

Larry Townsend was a giant of our leather archetribe and our gay culture. I miss the man still and forever. I loved him. He was wonderful. Let the academic studies begin. Let his books be kept in print. Let his novels be adapted into audiobooks and movies and long-form television series and stage plays. A suitable keening might be an hour spent reading from one of his novels like his epic of history, intrigue, and sadomasochism, *Czar! A Novel of Ivan the Terrible*.

On July 29 as he lay dying on that day we did not know he would die, Jeanne Barney wrote me at noon:

> At 11:43 a.m. we had a 5.8 magnitude earthquake. My desk, desk chair, computer, etc. bounced. Seussie barked, ran around in circles and was very frightened.

I responded minutes later at 12:02 PM:

Dear Jeanne, The earthquake is, one fantasizes, perhaps biblical, like the New Testament, when Christ died and there were earthquakes and the sky was darkened. The earth shakes on the day when Larry is very likely taken off his ventilator. As ever, Jack and Mark

Larry died at 2:40 PM.
Three days later on August 1, I commiserated:

Dear Jeanne, If the last 72 hours have been as hard on you as on us, may we hold hands? One can hardly think of LA without Larry Townsend there to keep things in order. What a character. No matter that he was often difficult, he was also human, and, ya know, forgive us our trespasses as we.… There's no denying the good comfort you gave him after Fred died. You were a good friend to him. If you two were too hot not to cool down, well, that's life. It's all "Musical Chairs." None of us knows if we will have a seat the next time the music stops. Keeping extremely busy with tons of work has been the best rite of grieving. As always, we are here for you, as we know you are for us. Love, Jack and Mark

Shortly thereafter, Jeanne, acting out her June 27 email predicting her imminent social withdrawal because of pain and depression, disappeared into her own re-framed new life in LA and died in 2019. What she left behind in her Arts and Crafts home at 1525 N. Gardner was, in the way gay history disappears, not archived, and was auctioned on eBay. Her home, one block off Sunset Boulevard, sold remodeled for $1,710,000 in 2020.

30

**HOLLYWOOD CELEBRITY HOMES BUS TOUR
THE TOWNSEND-YERKES HOUSE
1733 SUNSET PLAZA DRIVE
SPILL A DROP FOR LOST BROTHERS**

Thirteen years after Larry died, I was curious about whatever happened to the Townsend-Yerkes home. A quick search found their house completely remodeled in thirty-eight real-estate photos and in a 2017 YouTube tour of "1733 Sunset Plaza Drive." It was the house that porn built. If they weren't already dead, they would have died at the sight of the glass-and-steel mansion designed as a 3,000-square-foot luxury rental out of the wooden bones of the warm split-level bachelor-pad they kept carefully stuck in the 1970s. They had loved living in that Sunset Plaza celebrity enclave atop the Hollywood Hills five minutes above the Sunset Strip where they had made a home kept by their housekeeper and friend, Mark Decicco, who was helpful to them and to Larry's family after his passing.

Their house was ready for its close-up on the Celebrity Homes Open-Bus Tour. The photos pictured architectural updating that cut huge sliding windows into walls that could talk. I could feel Larry and Fred and evidence of their coupled existence ghosted behind the new design that will always be their haunt. It's a kick that the glamourous new look is imprinted with a gay literary and political history whose real-life gay Hollywood drama renters may never know. Just as there was a major Finnish feature film made about Tom of Finland in 2017, perhaps some new young screenwriter might lease the house to settle in, soak up the vibes, and write *The Larry Townsend Story* for Netflix.

Larry and Fred will always be alive and kicking in their kitchen and in their downstairs lounge-and-screening room with its gentleman's-club leather couches and its door to the outside stairs that led down to the dungeon; and in the northwest room that had been Larry's handsome office lined with framed photos that admiring fellow authors had sent him; and in their master bedroom where they slept together in a king-sized bed; and in their master bath where a whatnot shelf once hung in front of the mirror over the toilet tank reflecting to any man pissing their amusing collection of a hundred tiny porcelain pigs.

I fondly recall the kitchen where the lonesome widower, trying to keep on keeping on with his life by hosting guests like Mark and me, switched on his new blender to slush up some kind of raw pineapple-ice cocktail that, to much laughter, jumped and spewed all over him and us and his new marble counters and cabinets.

He was so proud that he, the leftover half of a Hollywood double act, had replaced their old kitchen table and chairs with six hand-carved blond Sudbury gothic side chairs and matching dining table mail-ordered from the quirky *Medieval and Gothic Catalog of Design Toscano*.

Online, in 2021, what a marvel to see the picture windows of their bedroom suite expanded into a Hollywood widescreen of floor-to-ceiling glass walls looking out over an infinity pool covering what had been Larry's tiny backyard torture garden described in the *Handbook*, Chapter 9, "Booze and Drugs." He wrote that privacy bushes surrounded his Hollywood back-lot scenes of psychodrama role play, of woodshed discipline, and of naked masochists staked out spreadeagle, turgid, and tits-up on the grass, or tied in languorous crucifixion to one of two T-shaped whipping posts originally dug in as laundry posts strung with white-cotton rope and spring-pin clothes pins so handy in S&M games.

The view looking southwest was still their view, but it had become an escalating five-million-dollar view stretching out across the lavender haze of West Hollywood and the smoggy towers of downtown Los Angeles to, like, you know, the fresh blue horizon of the rolling ocean.

Illustrations

Larry Townsend, Sebastopol, Sonoma County, California, June 16, 1995. Photo by Jack Fritscher

In 1972, Larry designed the first edition of *The Leatherman's Handbook* with a matte-black cover suggesting "leather," using a cargo-crate font suggesting "blue-collar" printed on a rectangle with cut corners suggesting a military "dog tag." To keep his books fresh for readers' eyes, he often created a succession of alternative covers for the same book. Born under the sign of Scorpio, he identified Kenneth Anger's *Scorpio Rising* (1963) as his favorite leather film. In 1974, he designed the second cover of his *Handbook* as an homage to Anger who spelled out on screen his two-word title in an arch of silver studs across the back of a leather jacket. Larry replaced Anger's arching *Scorpio* with *Leatherman's* and *Rising* with *Handbook*. Extant copies and images unavailable.

Larry Townsend, Sebastopol, Sonoma County, California, June 16, 1995. Photo by Jack Fritscher

Larry Townsend with Jeanne Barney and Jack Fritscher, the Los Angeles and San Francisco founding editors of *Drummer*, Dorothy Chandler Pavilion, Los Angeles, January 19, 2007. Photo by Mark Hemry (Back cover photo)

While writing for *The Advocate* in 1968, Larry met his "leather wife" Jeanne Barney, a staff founder of that magazine, whose advice column "Smoke from Jeannie's Lamp" moved to *Drummer* magazine when publisher John Embry, who founded *Drummer* all by himself in November 1971 and collaborated on it with Larry Townsend in 1972, hired her as editor from 1975 to 1976. Embry knew that Larry, whom he asked, should have been the founding LA editor-in-chief of *Drummer*, but alpha Larry said *no*. So alpha Embry chose Jeanne Barney who was more clerical and would bend to his will—until she didn't.

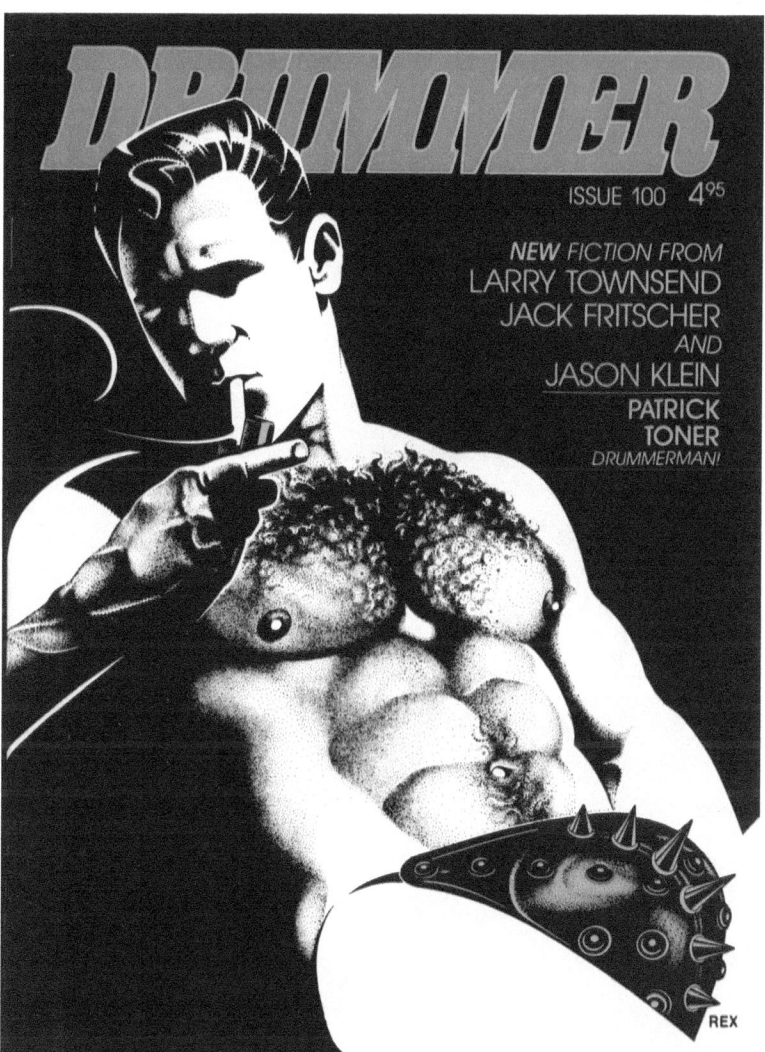

Tony DeBlase, the second publisher of *Drummer*, headlined Larry Townsend on the celebratory cover of the landmark issue, *Drummer* 100, November 1986. Drawing by Rex

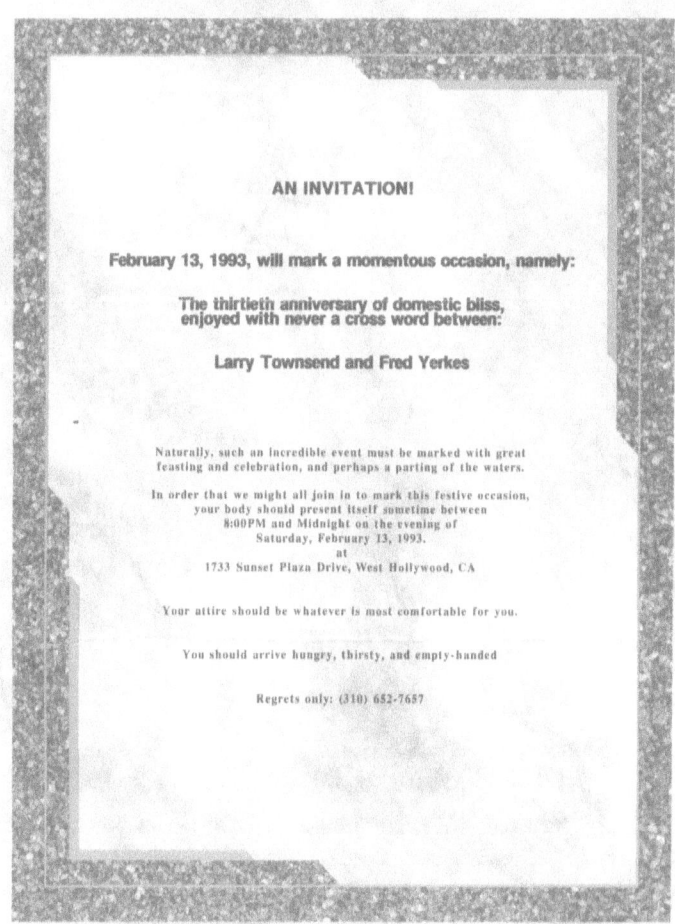

(Top left) "Do you two still have sex?" Larry Townsend and Fred Yerkes at night in the rain under the awning of the Irish Cottage, Town Square, Healdsburg, California, March 19, 1998. Photo by Jack Fritscher

(Bottom left) Mark Hemry, Larry Townsend, Jack Fritscher, Fred Yerkes, Bistro Ralph, Healdsburg, California, March 19, 1998.

(Above) Invitation, Townsend-Yerkes 30th Anniversary Party, Sunset Plaza Drive, Los Angeles, February 13, 1993. Larry announced: "The thirtieth anniversary of domestic bliss enjoyed with never a cross word between Larry Townsend and Fred Yerkes."

Irvin "Bud" Townsend Bernhard, Jr. age 25, Los Angeles, 1955. In this casual leather portrait, the tall slender "Bud," a commanding six-foot-one and 190 pounds, posed like a proper Marlon Brando and James Dean in khaki shirt with military epaulettes and black denim jeans with cuffs rolled up wide and big. This was his get-up in 1955 when he walked into his first leather bar, Cinema, on Melrose Avenue where the jukebox was playing the brand new rock-n-roll hit "Black Denim Trousers and Motorcycle Boots (and a Black Leather Jacket with an Eagle on the Back.") This was what he looked like in April 1955 when the Consul at the German Embassy in LA awarded the newly mustered-out Air Force Staff Sergeant a medal for saving a 9-year-old German boy from drowning in the Rhine River. On September 30, 1955, James Dean, who tooled around Hollywood on his 1955 Triumph Trophy, died young at 24—three months younger than Larry—in a car crash on a lonely California highway at dusk. Soon after, Larry sold his bike. (Front cover photo)

Irvin "Bud" Townsend Bernhard, Jr., self-portrait, age 20, 1950. Documenting his face the week before he enlisted in the U.S. Air Force to avoid the draft, Larry, whose father was a spy, served in military intelligence in post-war Germany where he toured the devastation, culture, and local talent on his motor scooter—and began his kinky adventures reading de Sade in the *Gemütlichkeit* of beer gardens similar to the one in the film *Cabaret* released the same year as *The Leatherman's Handbook*.

Larry Townsend, age 35, at home, Sunset Plaza Drive, Los Angeles, 1965. Art direction by Larry Townsend. Photo by Fred Yerkes

Larry Townsend with Doberman "Mueller" and "Slave Boy." Los Angeles, 1997. Photographer unknown. When invited that year to do a reading at A Different Light Bookstore on Castro Street in San Francisco, the star author waited until the audience was seated and made his grand entrance walking down the aisle to the podium with one leash on his Doberman and another leash on his slave. When both dog and slave "sat" at his stern command, he brought down the house with shouting and applause.

(Above) Larry Townsend, French Quarter Restaurant, West Hollywood, January 20, 2007. Photo by Jack Fritscher

(Top right) Larry Townsend with Doberman "Mueller," Sebastopol, California, June 16. 1995. Photo by Jack Fritscher

(Bottom right) Larry Townsend and Jack Fritscher, Sebastopol, California, June 16, 1995. Photo by Mark Hemry

Five co-creators on page and screen: Jeanne Barney, Jack Fritscher, and Larry Townsend with film producer Terry Legrand and director Roger Earl, the French Quarter Restaurant, West Hollywood, January 20, 2007. Photo by Mark Hemry

Larry Townsend with Jack Fritscher, Larry's friend Derrick, and Mark Hemry. Hotel Casa Del Mar, Santa Monica, California. June 1, 2008, shot during the last moments of the last parting of Townsend, Hemry, and Fritscher. Six weeks later, on July 13, Larry collapsed and Derrick drove him to Cedars-Sinai Hospital—three miles from his home, and two miles from the French Quarter restaurant—where he lay unconscious in Intensive Care until his passing on July 29, 2008.

Jeanne Barney, the controversial editor of *Drummer*, was intent on creating jobs for herself while breaking the glass ceiling in gay and straight male publishing. In an effort to syndicate herself during the Vietnam War in 1971 before there was much of a gay press, she began writing for the *Grunt Free Press*, the rag-paper alternative magazine full of military jokes, crude cartoons, and bare breasts for Vietnam veterans. Published in Agana, Guam, *Grunt* had an international circulation. Jeanne wanted to title her advice column in *Grunt* with the same title she was currently using in *The Advocate*, "Smoke from Jeannie's Lamp," but *The Advocate* said *no*; so she dubbed it "Genie Speaks," and used her legal name as her byline. In the first three issues of *Drummer*, her name did not appear on the masthead, even though she credited her first *Drummer* feature in issue one, "S&M: Out of the Closet and on to the Campus," with her own name.

(Top right) Chuck Arnett's "Portrait of Jeanne," Los Angeles, 1975. Used with permission.

Jack Fritscher 167

Drummer was a gender-positive magazine for masculine-identified men who liked men masculine in that first decade of gay lib when women were self-fashioning themselves in feminism. Diving into the male leather scene, Jeanne Barney made a demographic mistake when she published a Robert Opel photo of the Cycle Sluts on the Halloween 1976 cover of issue nine. Larry had warned her against promoting a show-biz act of bearded men in *Rocky Horror Show* drag. Subscribers complained about gender-benders infiltrating a brand new male-sanctuary magazine. Her miscalculation, disrupting the very leather homomasculinity that took her under its wing, unseated her authenticity with readers. Two issues later, it wasn't cause and effect exactly, but she quit as editor. She claimed Embry owed her $13,000 in back pay.

(Top and bottom) The Townsend-Yerkes lounge and screening room where Fred Yerkes died unexpectedly late at night on July 7, 2006, while watching television alone. Larry woke and found him just before dawn on the couch next to the life-size King Tut Sarcophagus situated in the corner (bottom photo, upper left) among their collected books and curios, January 21, 2007. Photo by Mark Hemry

(Top) King Tut curios and Larry Townsend's home display of his books in their lounge and screening room, January 21, 2007. Photo by Mark Hemry

(Bottom) Larry Townsend at his writing desk in his book-lined study, January 21, 2007. Photo by Mark Hemry

(Top and bottom) Larry Townsend at his writing desk in his study working on an early draft of his last novel, *TimeMasters*, January 21, 2007. Photo by Mark Hemry

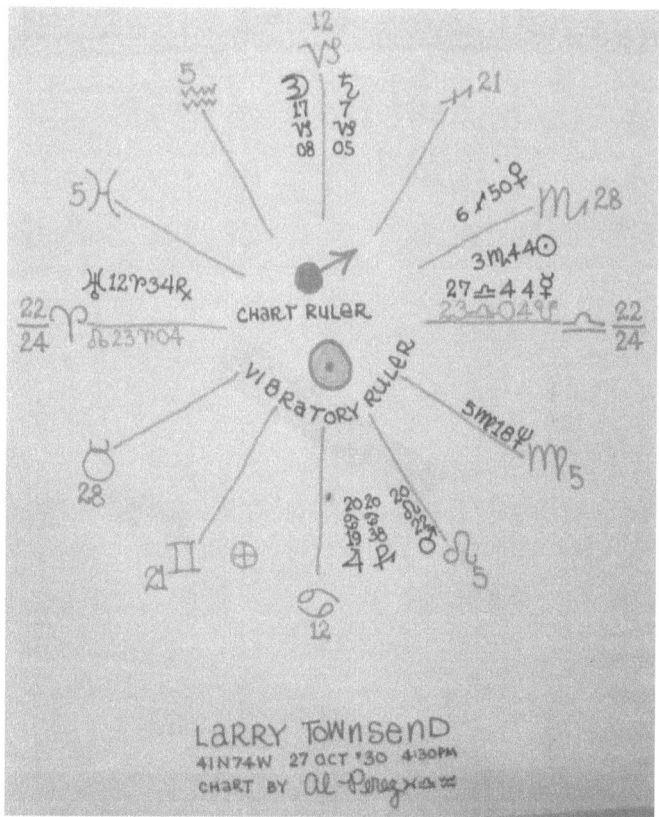

A 1970s astrology chart for the adult "Larry Townsend" came years after the horoscope his mother bought for "Irvin Townsend Bernhard, Jr.," after his 4:30 pm birth October 27, 1930, which read: "December 18, 1930... After studying your name... you're a lucky boy! Men in your group frequently become financial and scientific leaders. I do hope you won't neglect your splendid abilities. You have good judgement, a fine mind, wisdom beyond your years, tolerance toward the views of others... but I urge you not to get in the habit of tyrannizing over your friends.... You like to see people and money working for you.... Your name and destiny combination...should not be changed.... Petty trifles annoy you...Your type... often marry after 25.... Do not change your name. Sincerely, Lorna Fantin"

As happened, in spite of the astrologer's warning, "Irvin-'Bud'-Townsend-Bernhard-Junior-Michael-Lawrence-'Larry' Townsend" changed his name, became a star, and left a cultural legacy of writing, art, and photography.

"Spill a Drop for Lost Brothers," obituary for Larry Townsend by Jack Fritscher published in *The Leather Times* magazine of the Leather Archives & Museum, Chicago, 2008. Winner of the 2009 National Leather Association International: "Cynthia Slater Non-Fiction Feature Article Award."

In 1996, for the 25th Anniversary edition of *The Leatherman's Handbook*, Larry invited Jack Fritscher to write a new introduction titled "I Am Curious (Leather): Leather Dolce Vita, Pop Culture, and the Prime of Mr. Larry Townsend."

Jack Fritscher 173

"Leather Legend Larry Townsend Dies," obituary for Larry Townsend by Jack Fritscher published in Dave Rhodes' *The Leather Journal*, September 2008, Los Angeles.

(Above) In addition to his 1955 award from the German government for saving a boy drowning in the Rhine River, Larry was honored with many trophies including a "Lifetime Achievement Award" from LeatherFest Los Angeles in 1995.

(Top right) In 1995, he won both the "Steve Maidhof Award" for activist literature as well as a "Lifetime Achievement Award" from the National Leather Association-International.

(Bottom right) In 2000, he received the "Special Community Award" from Christopher Street West.

In 2002, Larry was celebrated with the Pantheon of Leather "Forebear Award" sponsored by Dave Rhodes' *Leather Journal*.

In 2002, he received the Obelisk "Lifetime Achievement Award" from the Erotic Authors Association. The photograph of the transparent-glass Obelisk Award was shot to show the view of LA from his bedroom window.

In 2016, the Cleveland Leather Annual Weekend inducted him posthumously into the CLAW "Leather Hall of Fame."

The first issue of the *H.E.L.P, Inc. Newsletter*, September 15, 1970. In 1968 Larry Townsend helped found "H.E.L.P., the Homophile Effort for Legal Protection" to bail out and defend gays during and after entrapment arrests by the Los Angeles Police Department. He was the founding editor of the *H.E.L.P.Newsletter* and served on the board of directors. In 1972, Larry became president of H.E.L.P and was arrested by the LAPD at the H.E.L.P. fundraiser he hosted at the Black Pipe leather bar.

Data-boy, Volume 2, No. 10, March 3, 1971. As a crusading political columnist, Larry wrote about gay liberation, gay character, and police brutality in dozens of political columns in dozens of gay pop-culture publications such as *The Advocate, Vector, Drummer, Honcho, Entertainment West, California Scene, H.E.L.P. Incorporated Newsletter,* and *Data-boy.*

In 1973, the *H.E.L.P.Newsletter* was renamed *H.E.L.P.Drummer* and became a prototype of the glossy *Drummer* magazine founded in LA in 1975 by Larry's forever frenemy, John Embry, who in a smooth move deposed Larry as H.E.L.P. president. *The Advocate* reported on April 25, 1973, that some members thought the election was rigged and that it was inappropriate that a non-profit legal-aid organization was being used to create Embry's commercial magazine.

County of Los Angeles
Office of the Sheriff
Hall of Justice
Los Angeles, California 90012

PETER J. PITCHESS, SHERIFF

October 7, 1971

Larry Townsend, Vice President
Publications Director
H.E.L.P., Incorporated
P. O. Box 3007
Hollywood, California 90028

Dear Mr. Townsend:

I appreciate very much your kind words regarding our meeting of September 13, 1971 in my office. It is through such conferences that we in law enforcement are best able to determine the feelings of our community and the social problems which exist therein.

I have had an opportunity to discuss your suggestion regarding our West Hollywood Station with Inspector Lanier, and he joins me in thinking that perhaps a more appropriate answer would be to establish a link of communications between members of your organization and the personnel of this Department who are most closely associated with enforcement policies in your particular area of concern. I have asked Inspector Lanier to coordinate such meetings and request that you communicate your thoughts on this matter directly to him.

Sincerely,

Peter J. Pitchess

PETER J. PITCHESS
SHERIFF

Involved in politics for forty years, Townsend wrote hundreds of letters to city and county officials seeking a truce between the LAPD and the gay community.

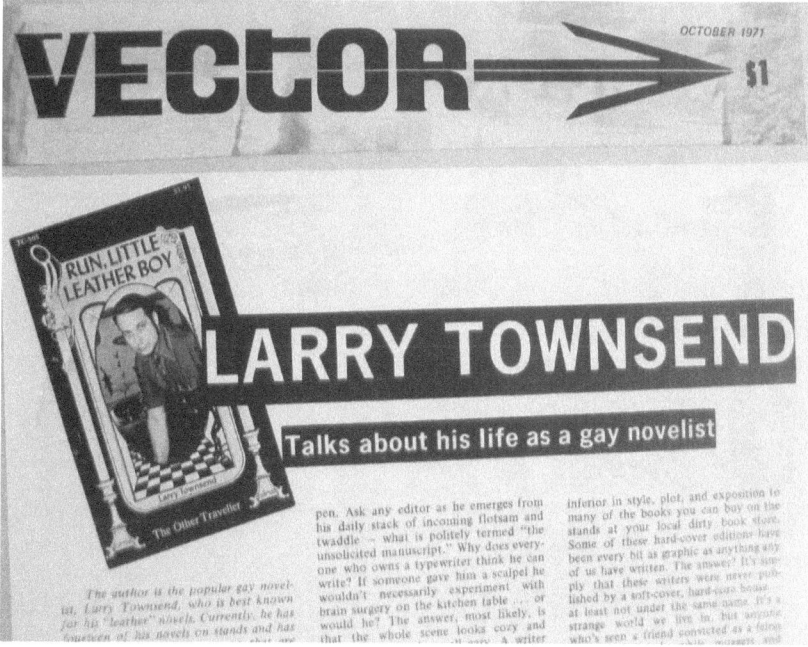

As a public person, Larry guarded his privacy which ended in 1972 with the publication of his wildly popular *The Leatherman's Handbook*. Over the years, he often said that his signature book had sold more than a hundred thousand copies in a gay publishing market where "5,000 copies sold" constitutes a best-seller. His first personal interview, "Larry Townsend Talks about His Life as a Gay Novelist," was published in the San Francisco magazine, *Vector*, October 1971. His last was in publisher Bob Wingate's *Bound and Gagged*, January/February, 1993, issue 32.

(Above) *California Scene*, January 1972. Larry received starry billing with Christopher Isherwood and Bob Damron headlined with gay novelist Douglas Dean. Townsend and Dean had become friends at the first meeting of gay porn authors in San Francisco in 1970 when Larry advised the writers how to organize against publishers who ripped them off. The text is laid across a drawing of the "Leather David" statue designed in 1966 by gay novelist Sam Steward and created by sculptor Mike Caffee for Febe's leather bar on Folsom Street in San Francisco.

(Right) In 1972, Larry exited the Republican party and became the president of the Hollywood Hills Democratic Club, the first openly gay political club in LA. As an activist, he received a letter of gratitude from celebrity attorney, Democrat Vincent Bugliosi, prosecutor of Charles Manson, and the author of *Helter-Skelter*, for donating to his campaign to become LA District Attorney—an election Bugliosi lost before going on to a successful writing career.

SEEN AT A RECENT POLITICAL MEETING: Writer Larry Townsend and President of the Hollywood Hills Democratic Club with lawyer Vince Bugliosi, aspirant to the post of State Attorney General in the forthcoming elections.

Politics & You

WHY THE DEMOCRATIC PARTY?
by Larry Townsend

VINCENT T. BUGLI...

Mr. Michael Townsend
P. O. Box 302
Beverly Hills, California
90213

Dear Mr. Townsend:

Please accept my personal thanks f... campaign. I am convinced that wit... interested people like yourself we... a successful conclusion in Novembe...

As you know, as District Attorney I... priorities and represent every citi... not just the privileged few. Your... significant contribution toward acc...

Again, thank you very much.

Best personal regards,

Vincent T. Bugliosi
Vincent T. Bugliosi

VTB/bjs

The Advocate, Issue 94, September 13, 1972. In 1972, the LAPD busted Larry's H.E.L.P. fundraiser at the Black Pipe leather bar on La Cienega Boulevard. The cops arrested 21 leathermen, including Larry, the president of H.E.L.P, who was booked under both his names. The charge was "Lewd Conduct" because one of the booths on the outdoor patio auctioned off leathermen for a date to raise money to open a gay Community Center. The LAPD declared this was prostitution.

Police Chief Ed Davis ordered the attack because of Larry's activism and the fact that Black Pipe bar was owned by Dwayne Moller, the chairman of the Tavern Guild police resistance in LA. After great emotional and financial distress, the "Black Pipe 21" were finally cleared of charges on June 21, 1974. The fiasco cost Larry more than two thousand dollars. This 1972 police raid was a dress rehearsal for the raid on the Drummer Slave Auction in 1976.

H.E.L.P.Drummer, Volume 2, No. 2, October 15, 1972. On the cover, editor Townsend, a master of marketing synergy, reported on the local bar, street, and political scene while headlining a column promoting his newest novel, *Run No More*, the sequel to his best-selling *Run, Little Leather Boy*. Everything the canny businessman did had a marketing angle that led to the success of his publishing company which was one of the first gay-owned small businesses that wasn't a bar.

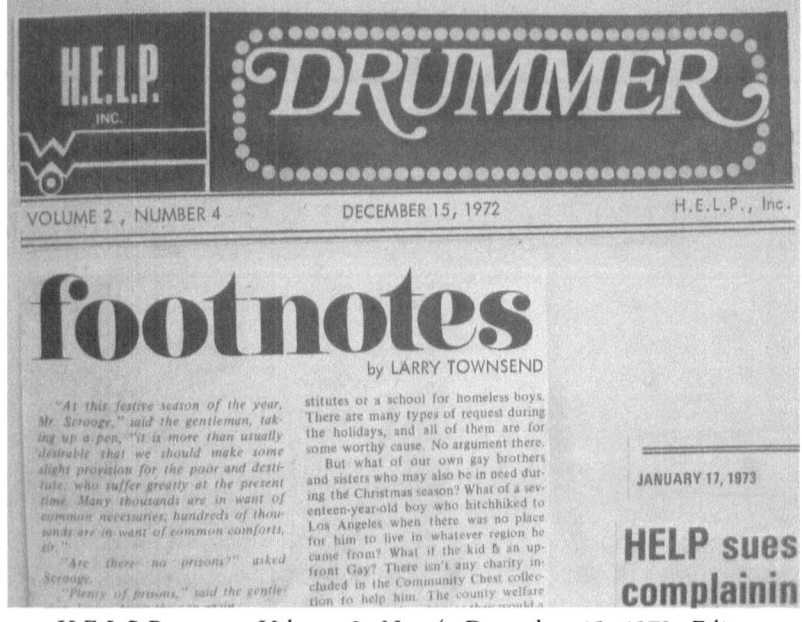

H.E.L.P.Drummer, Volume 2, No. 4, December 15, 1972. Editor Townsend's Christmas editorial called for community care of the young gay runaways living unhoused and hustling on the streets of LA.

The Advocate, March 28, 1973. "Now You Listen to Me." At a February 22 hearing that "turned into a shouting match," Larry Townsend (sporting new sideburns) exchanged words with LA city councilman Robert J. Stevenson, a former actor and early supporter of gay rights who represented District 13 Hollywood-Silver Lake-Highland Park. Stevenson's 1974 proposal to make job discrimination against gays illegal was stopped by the anti-gay LAPD Police Chief Ed Davis who hated *Drummer,* bugged its office phones, and assigned detectives to follow the staff in cars.

MAYOR-CANDIDATE TOM BRADLEY HELD A NEWS CONFERENCE for Gay Media and Community Representatives in the H.E.L.P. Center just outside the DRUMMER office. Pictured facing candidate Bradley are (l. to r.) Drummer columnist Jim Kepner (also President of ONE, Inc.), Advocate News Editor Robb Cole, Marty Butel of G.C.A., Attorney Albert Gordon, Publicist Baxter Lowery, Jay Morley of A.C.L.U., H.E.L.P. President Larry Townsend and Drummer Editor John Embry.

Kepner (also President of ONE, Inc.), Advocate News Editor Robb Cole, Marty Butel of G.C.A., Attorney Albert Gordon, Publicist Baxter Lowery, Jay Morley of A.C.L.U., H.E.L.P. President Larry Townsend and Drummer Editor John Embry.

(Top: full image. Bottom: detail of image) *The Advocate*, 1973. Campaigning to become mayor of Los Angeles, African-American candidate Tom Bradley held a news conference at the H.E.L.P. headquarters. Pictured left to right: Jim Kepner, President of ONE, Inc; Rob Cole, founder of *The Advocate*; straight attorney Albert Gordon, the legendary defender of arrested leatherfolk; publicist Baxter Lowery; Jay Motley of the ACLU; the suave H.E.L.P. president Larry Townsend posing like a screen star owning the focus of the photo; and *Drummer* editor, John Embry. With LGBT support, Bradley became the 38th Mayor of Los Angeles (1973 to 1993). Photo by Walt Blumoff

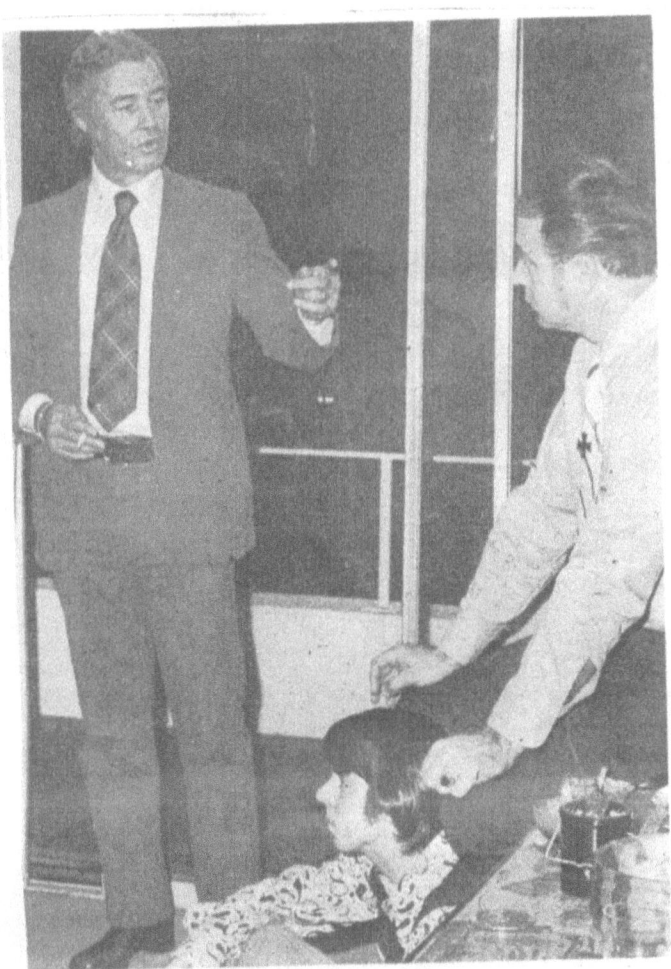

The Advocate, April 11, 1973. "Pledges Aid. State Sen. George Mosconi [*sic*; actually *Moscone*] (D-San Francisco) [who would be assassinated alongside Harvey Milk in 1978] speaks at a cocktail party in the Los Angeles home of outgoing H.E.L.P. President Larry Townsend (right) and Fred Yerkes Friday, Mar. 9. The get-together was arranged through the Alice B. Toklas Memorial Democratic Club of San Francisco and was co-hosted by Jim Foster, president of the club. "The gay community need a champion," said Mosconi [*sic*], and he pledged to act as such if he is successful in his campaign for governor of California in 1974. Sitting on the floor is Frank Zerilli of Gay Community Alliance." Photo by Walt Blumoff

"*The Advocate*, May 23, 1973. Press Conference. W. Dorr Legg, founder of ONE, Inc., makes a point at a press conference held by Gays at the Los Angeles Press Club April 27 to denounce what they called an attack on the gay community by City Attorney Roger Arnebergh [who, as a result of gay opposition would lose in the next election]. Others in the photo are H.E.L.P. President John Embry (left), former H.E.L.P. President Larry Townsend, and Tom Coleman (at right) of Gay Law Students Assn." Photo by Walt Blumoff

In 1972, six months before this photo was taken, Townsend's and Embry's names appeared together for the first time on the masthead of the first issue of the newsprint magazine combining Townsend's *H.E.L.P.Newsletter* with advertising salesman Embry's small zine-version of *Drummer* which Embry had first published all by his lonesome in November 1971. The new title was *H.E.L.P.Drummer*. The merger flopped because in 1973, Embry displaced Larry as president of H.E.L.P. Larry stayed aboard as an ex-officio member of the H.E.L.P. board of directors.

> Page 8   THE ADVOCATE   DECEMBER 4, 1974
>
> # *We, the people...*
> by LARRY TOWNSEND
>
> ## how many more negative mandates?
>
> Politics, sweet politics . . . and who cares? It's over for another couple of years, at least nationally, and the intervening local elections are even less exciting—or so I keep hearing 'em say, out there.
> So while the discredited old guard "69;" you do for me, and I'll do for you. So while we look to make the necessary contacts, to seek the commitments and to educate these candidates to our needs, we must also consider the pragmatic realities. Our contact person must be a man Americana. We are just as frightened as anyone else by the spectre of depression, recession, and economic collapse. The person who is going to speak for us should understand this; preferably, he or she should have been there.

The Advocate, December 4, 1974. Larry Townsend was an action-driven novelist who for years wrote activist-driven journalism in dozens of papers like *The Advocate* to rally leatherfolk against the gay civil war over gender and the takeover of gay culture by left-wing radicals of the Gay Liberation Front and the Socialist Workers Party (SWP). In *H.E.L.P.Drummer*, March 1973, Larry wrote:

> The leftists have always been there, of course, but it has been quite awhile since we have seen them in all their malicious glory. Over the weekend of February 3rd, at the California Committee for Sexual Law Reform Convention (H.E.L.P. Center), the rock was lifted and out they came! Following the time-honored tactic of the Socialist Workers' Party, their unspoken battle cry was: "*Take it over if you can, and if you can't—Destroy it!*" [Italics his]

Militants from the SWP shot back against "the sexist gay male press," specifically slamming gay male pioneers Larry; Jim Kepner, ONE, Inc.; and Rob Cole, founder of *The Advocate*, in *The Lesbian Tide*, April 1973, Volume 2, Number 9.

Larry was one of those alpha people who speak straight from the shoulder and straight from the heart, but he never told anyone what to do. He never canceled anyone.

MailBag

Alpha is 'most filthy piece of trash'

Editor:

In perusing Issue 86 of the AD-VOCATE and noting with interest the partial alleviation of the news blackout of progressive gay programs, witnessed in those publications "catering" to the homosexual populace, I was shocked to see the most filthy piece of trash (page 12) to be found anywhere.

I refer to the cartoon strip entitled "Alpha and the Scorpians." This has got to be the most miserable obscenity to ever feed the jaded lusts of those who have pushed the theory that Gays are "sick."

While I count myself foremost in the defense of the freedom of speech, such material as you have "exhibited" here has no relationship (fictional or otherwise) to what gay people are in reality. It stands us a direct slap in the face of over and beyond the majority of our peoples. I would hope that our gay sisters would rise to denounce such prurient commer-

cialization of garbage.

With all the respect I have toward Mr. Townsend, I am dismayed that he would divide his energies within the gay community to producing the basis for such material. We have here a series depicting gay people (presumably) as idiotic, abnormally developed physical specimens "flying" about in space.

I sincerely hope that we will be spared from such, particularly considering that progress and news cannot be divorced from the already gross and sexist advertising found rampant.

Lee Ellingworth-Wilson
Spokesman, GAA/L.A.
Los Angeles

> The ADVOCATE welcomes expressions of opinion from its readers on any subject of interest to the homophile community. Please be brief and to the point. The name and phone number of the writer must be on each letter for verification. Phone numbers will NOT be printed. Names are withheld IF THE WRITER REQUESTS IT. Send to Letters Dept., ADVOCATE, Box 74695, Los Angeles 90004.

In 1972, *The Advocate* in a burst of pop-culture camp—before its second publisher David Goodstein made it uptight about outlaw leather culture—so liked Larry Townsend's *The Scorpius Equation*, it turned his novel into the gay cartoon strip, *Alpha and the Scorpions*. Vanilla subscribers complained it was "a most filthy piece of trash"—which was a wonderful review.

Mineshaft Nights. Larry Townsend was as much a media celebrity in London and Berlin and Chicago as he was in Los Angeles. In New York at the Mineshaft on February 28, 1982, manager Wally Wallace feted him like a leather god with a party invitation drawn by Rex who threw down a gauntlet to the guests with a message advising: "The very best way to tell our guest Larry Townsend... that New York knows what he wrote about is to just get down and do it!" Ironic. Fans may have thought his fiction was autobiography, but he was there to sell books. He talked and wrote a good game, but he never joined the joy at the perversatile Mineshaft because he was not a heavy player and was not into drugs. He knew the private Townsend could never measure up to the public Townsend.

When *Drummer* was ten-months old, the LAPD raided the *Drummer* charity Slave Auction at the Mark IV Bath on April 10, 1976, when forty-two leatherfolk were arrested for prostitution and breaking a 19th-century law forbidding slavery. When the cops handcuffed Jeanne, they asked her if she was a drag queen. She said, "If I were a drag queen, I'd have bigger tits." Larry, whom the LAPD had arrested at the Black Pipe bar slave-auction fundraiser in 1972, was not present. He told leather author, Jack Rinella: "Fortunately for me we [Embry and he] had a falling out before the Slave Auction. Otherwise, I would have been there and would probably been arrested [along with Embry, Jeanne, Terry Legrand, and Roger Earl]. We [Embry and he] had a terrible squabble." The Slave Auction bust was so traumatic that *Drummer* fled from disaster in Los Angeles to destiny in San Francisco.

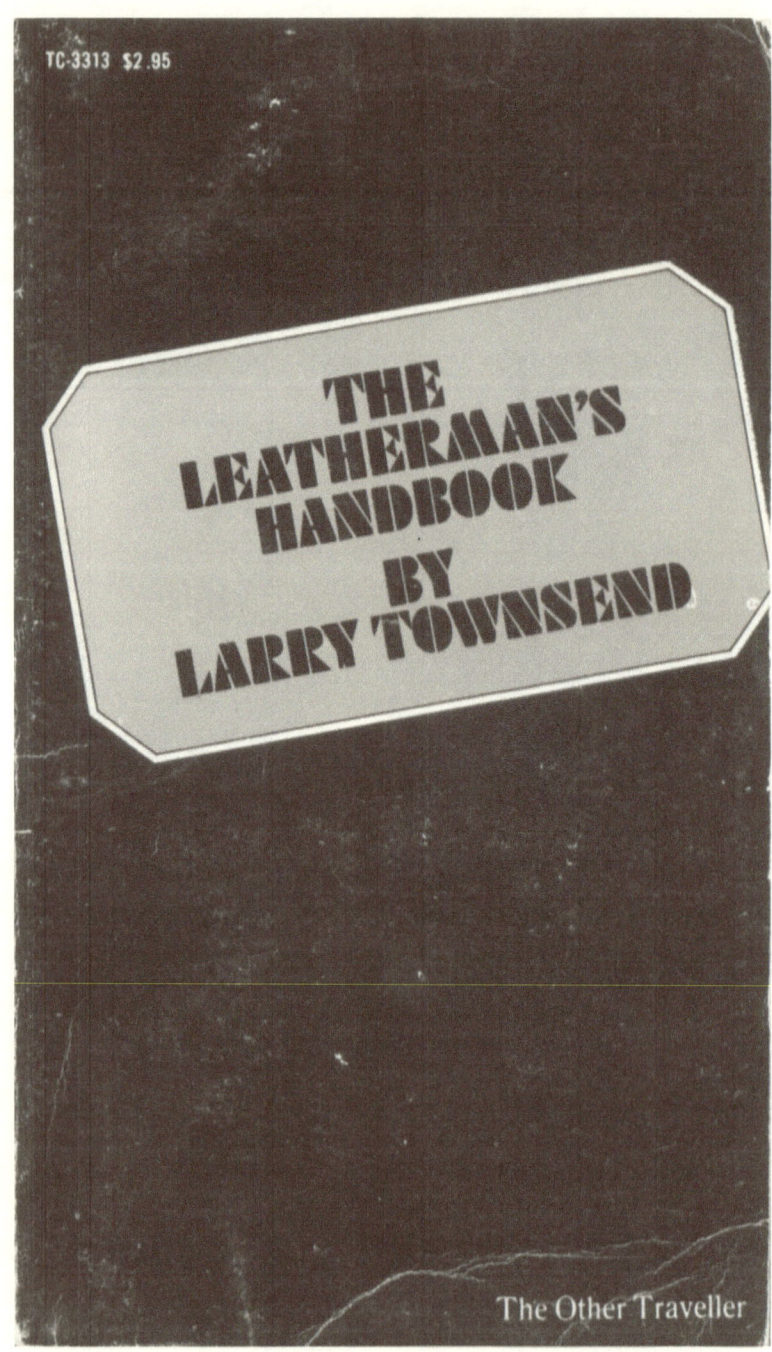

Jack Fritscher 197

> LE SALON, 30 SHERIDAN STREET, SAN FRANCISCO, CA 94103
> presents
>
> # THE LEATHERMAN'S HANDBOOK
> ## BY LARRY TOWNSEND
>
> The International Best Seller — Now in Its Third Printing!
> Complete Original Text with Updated Glossaries
>
> The only definitive exploration of the gay S&M leather scene ever written by a qualified writer who has observed it all from the inside. A nostalgic trip for the advanced practitioner, a "must" for the novice, the **HANDBOOK** contains:
>
> **THE FIRST** published statistics on S&M preferences...
>
> **THE FIRST** comprehensive listing of leather bars and leather suppliers in the United States, Canada and Europe...
>
> **THE FIRST** intimate account of in-group customs and mores.
>
> **THE FIRST** honest appraisal of the S&M personality, both in the blackroom and in the social world of leather.
>
> Written by the most widely acclaimed author in the field of the S&M leather novel, **THE LEATHERMAN'S HANDBOOK** tells you where to look for it, what to do and how to do it, once you find what you're after!
>
> Softbound, $3.95 ($4.45 1st Class or Canada)
>
> LE SALON, 30 Sheridan Street, San Francisco, CA 94103
>
> Please send ____ copies of THE LEATHERMAN'S HANDBOOK.
>
> I enclose $ ____ ($3.95 each; $4.45 1st Class or Canada)
>
> Name: ____
> Address: ____
> City: ____ State: ____ Zip: ____
> I am 21 years of age or over:
> Signature: ____

The Leatherman's Handbook full-page ad helped make *Drummer* 21 a platonic ideal of what a perfect issue of *Drummer* could be (March 1978). Larry's grassroots artwork was the same "trade secret" as the low-tech hands-on art design of *Drummer* itself which was calculated to give the writing, art, and photography a sense of real people creating and contributing and sharing their real experiences of leather *verite* that corporate plastic publishing could not offer in the Mafia-supported gay magazines.

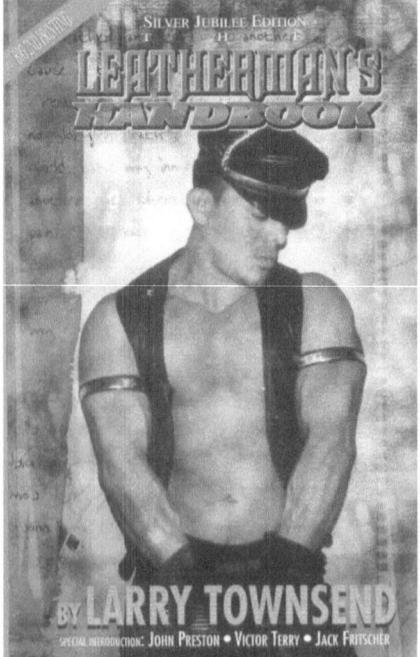

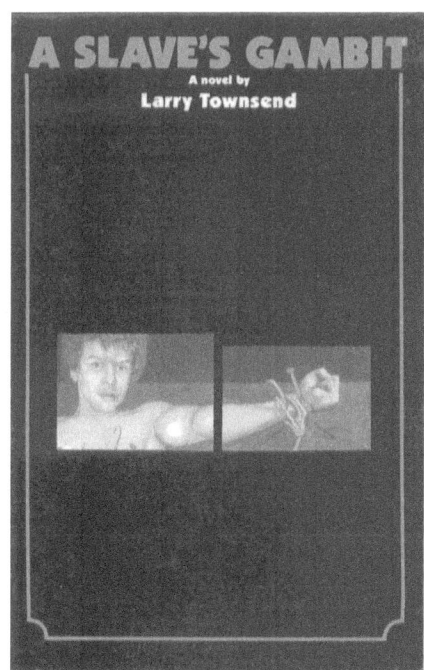
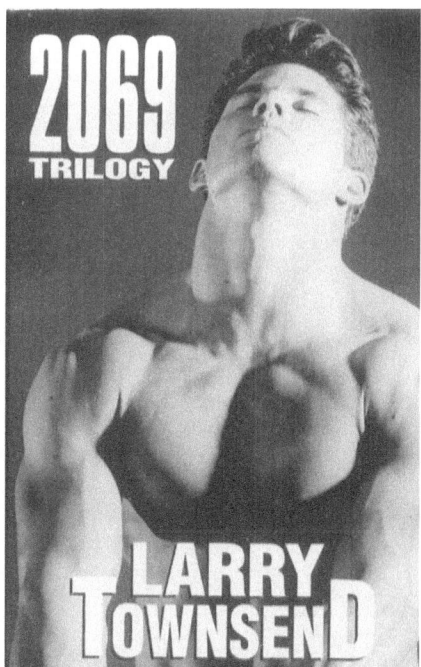

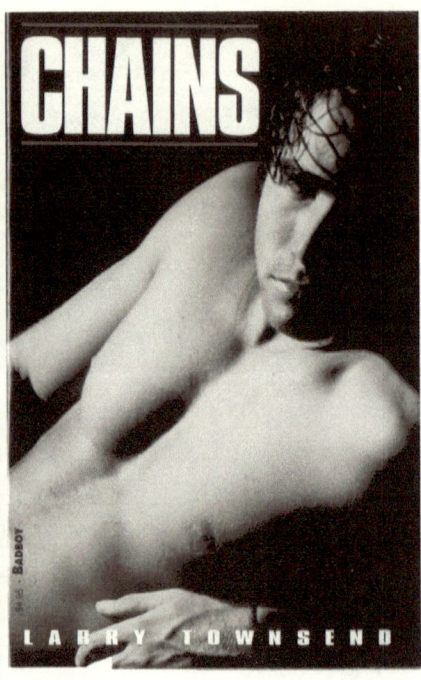

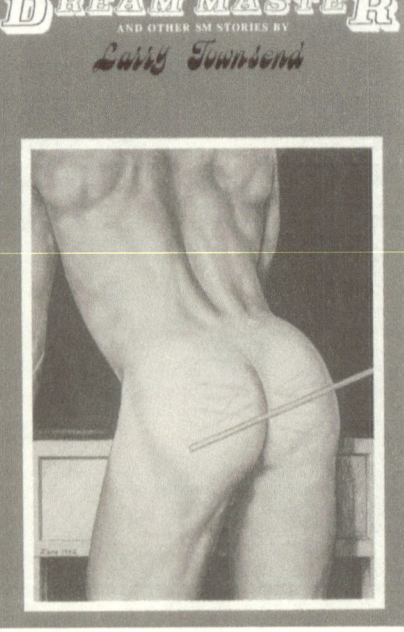

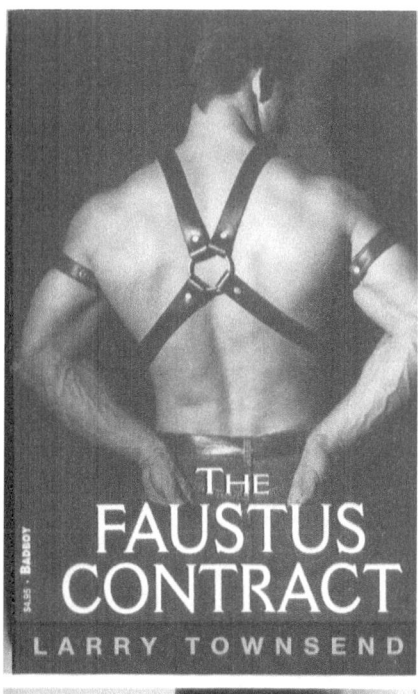

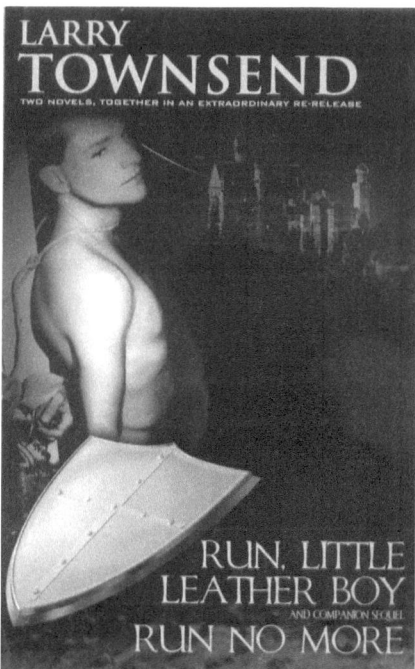
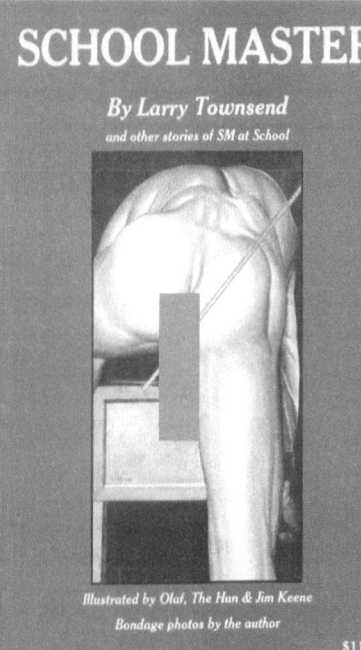
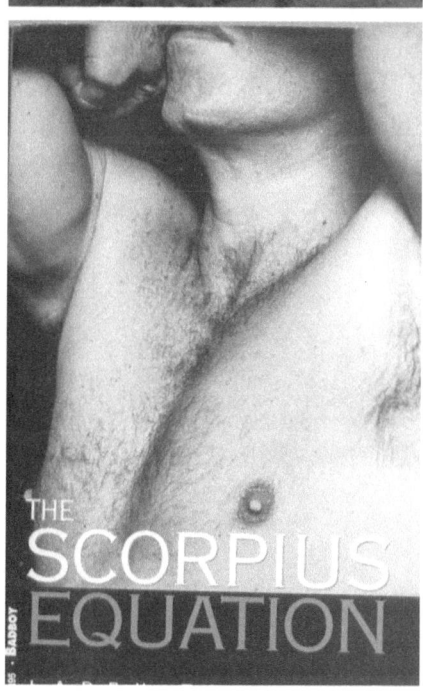

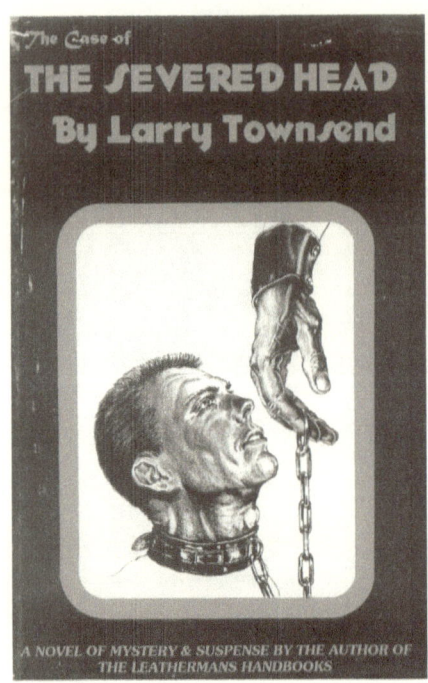
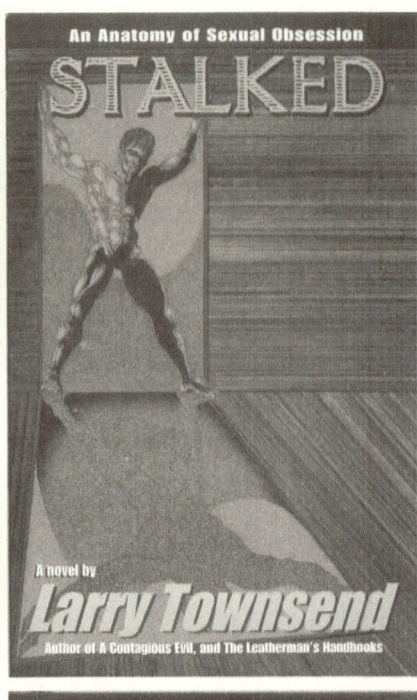

Other Works by Jack Fritscher

Novels

Some Dance to Remember
The Geography of Women
What They Did to the Kid
Leather Blues

Short-Fiction

Rainbow County
Corporal in Charge
Stand by Your Man
Titanic
Stonewall: Stories of Gay Liberation
Sweet Embraceable You

Non-Fiction

Gay San Francisco: Eyewitness Drummer
Gay Pioneers
Mapplethorpe: Assault with a Deadly Camera
Popular Witchcraft
Love and Death in Tennessee Williams
When Malory Met Arthur: Camelot
Television Today

www.JackFritscher.com

www.ingramcontent.com/pod-product-compliance
Lightning Source LLC
Chambersburg PA
CBHW021145080526
44588CB00008B/220